CULTURES OF THE WORLD®

DENMARK

Robert Pateman

MARSHALL CAVENDISH BENCHMARK

NEW YORK

PICTURE CREDITS

Cover: © Royalty-Free/Corbis

Bes Stock: 5, 130 • Corbis, Inc.: 13, 32, 43, 44, 45, 46 • HBL Network: 3, 12, 24, 34, 65, 69, 76, 89, 90, 108 • The Hulton-Deutsch Collection: 18, 21, 36, 80, 86, 94, 95 • The Hutchison Library: 23, 35, 40, 56, 64, 81 • The Image Bank: 8, 14, 15, 16, 17, 19, 28, 82, 109, 111, 114, 124 • International Photobank: 16, 26 • Life File Photographic Library: 7, 11, 22, 29, 30, 31, 32, 33, 50, 53, 55, 57, 58, 61, 62, 63, 68, 83, 84, 88, 92, 96, 98, 101, 106, 107, 115, 119, 120, 122, 125, 126, 127, 128 • Lonely Planet Images: 1, 6, 9, 42, 47, 48, 62, 76, 84, 104, 120 • Robert Pateman: 4, 10, 51, 67, 70, 72, 73, 75, 85, 93, 97, 121, 129 • Photobank Singapore: 41 • Reuters: 49, 50, 92, 112 • Royal Danish Tourism Board: 105, 118 • David Simson: 26, 37, 39, 54, 60, 71, 78, 91, 103, 110, 112 • Stock Food / Iden. K.: 131

PRECEDING PAGE

An urban Danish crowd

Marshall Cavendish Benchmark
99 White Plains Road
Tarrytown, NY 10591
Website: www.marshallcavendish.us

© Times Editions Private Limited 1995
© Marshall Cavendish International (Asia) Private Limited 2006
All rights reserved. First edition 1995. Second edition 2006.
® "Cultures of the World" is a registered trademark of Times Publishing Limited.

Originated and designed by Times Editions
An imprint of Marshall Cavendish International (Asia) Private Limited
A member of Times Publishing Limited

All Internet sites were correct and accurate at the time of printing.

Library of Congress Cataloging-in-Publication Data
Pateman, Robert, 1954–
    Denmark / by Robert Pateman. – 2nd ed.
       p. cm. – (Cultures of the world)
    Includes bibliographical references and index.
    Summary: "Provides comprehensive information on the geography, history, governmental structure,
       economy, cultural diversity, peoples, religion, and culture of Denmark" – Provided by publisher.
    ISBN 0-7614-2024-X
    1. Denmark—Juvenile literature. I. Title. II. Series.
    DL109.P37 2006
    948.9--dc22   2005021610

Printed in China

7 6 5 4 3 2 1

CONTENTS

A Danish symbol of manual labor includes a windmill and Danish flag.

A street painting in Copenhagen.

INTRODUCTION

DENMARK IS A SMALL COUNTRY in northern Europe. It is almost entirely surrounded by water, and the sea influences many aspects of Danish life. A thousand years ago, some of the Danes were fierce Viking warriors who sailed in long ships, causing terror in Europe. Today the Danes are a peaceful people who enjoy one of the highest standards of living in the world.

Denmark conjures up many different images: the Little Mermaid statue in Copenhagen, rolling farmland, the royal guards in their immaculate red uniforms, and the Danish flag, the Dannebrog. Behind these visual symbols of the nation lies a private side of Denmark that is more difficult to explore. A sense of humor, close family ties, national pride, and happy evenings spent enjoying good food with friends are equally important elements of Danish culture.

However, many Danes have concerns about the future. Some wonder how environmental issues will affect their small country. Immigration is another major issue, and many Danes supported an "anti-immigration" policy in the 2005 election that conflicted with the country's reputation for being liberal and open.

GEOGRAPHY

PART OF NORTHERN EUROPE, Denmark covers 16,639 square miles (43,094 square km), which is about twice the size of Massachusetts. It is made up of the narrow Jutland Peninsula and over 400 islands. No place in Denmark is farther than 32 miles (52 km) from the sea.

Jutland is joined to mainland Europe by a 42-mile (67-km) land border with Germany. It makes up about two-thirds of Denmark's land area. The soil here is generally poor and long ago was covered with moor, heath, and sand dunes. Today the use of modern fertilizers enables extensive farming in Jutland. The islands are generally far more fertile. The most typical features are low rolling hills, lakes, and beaches. The Danish capital, Copenhagen, is situated on the island of Zealand.

Left: **Rold Forest is Denmark's biggest forest. The country was once covered with deciduous forest.**

Opposite: **Rape fields in West Zealand.**

Rolling hills meet a beach in northern Zealand.

PHYSICAL FEATURES

Denmark is generally a flat country. This is the result of the glaciers that pushed across the land during the ice ages. Undulating plains alternate with gently rolling hills. A line of low hills running north to south through the Jutland Peninsula clearly mark the farthest point of the most recent glacier advance. The highest point, Yding Skovhøj in eastern Jutland, is 568 feet (173 m) above sea level. Another legacy of the ice ages are the countless small lakes and streams. Arresø in northern Zealand is the biggest of the lakes, covering 15.7 square miles (40.8 square km).

Dune landscapes form an almost unbroken belt along the western coast of Jutland. The western dune coast has many sandy beaches and fjords. The calm waters of the fjords make them favorite places for Denmark's yachts. There are two major fjords: Lim Fjord in Jutland and Ise Fjord in Zealand. The long Danish coastline has a great number of gulfs, inlets, and lagoons that contain brackish (somewhat salty) water.

CLIMATE

Denmark's climate is strongly influenced by the sea. Thanks to the warm North Atlantic Drift, which is part of the Gulf Stream, the weather is often mild for a country at such a high latitude. Being surrounded by water means Denmark receives a heavy rainfall, averaging about 25 inches (64 cm) a year. Jutland is generally the wettest part of the country; this area can receive over 30 inches (76 cm) of annual precipitation.

The lack of mountains has another strong influence on the weather. It means that winds blowing in from the sea can quickly sweep across the whole country. As a result, it is unusual to find the weather differing very much from one part of Denmark to another.

A frozen forest landscape on the island of Sjaelland in West Zealand.

This red squirrel must hibernate to avoid the harsh Danish winter.

FLORA AND FAUNA

Most of Denmark was originally covered by deciduous forest, the most common trees being beech, oak, elm, and lime. Virtually all the original forest was chopped down several centuries ago. Today approximately 12 percent of Denmark is covered with trees, but these are mostly replanted forests. In Jutland many of the new plantations are of coniferous trees such as spruce and fir, which grow in areas that were once open heath.

Such drastic human interference has had a major effect on the wildlife, and over the centuries many mammal species have disappeared from Denmark. These include bear, boar, wolves, and elk, some of which have found shelter in the more northerly regions of Scandinavia. Today the largest mammal in Denmark is the red deer. Smaller mammals are still common and include several species of bats, red squirrels, hares, and hedgehogs.

Denmark is home to around 300 species of birds. The long coastline with its many inlets and gulfs provides a particularly rich home for water birds, including herons, swans, and storks. Storks play an important role in Danish folklore and are believed to bring good luck. Although they are strictly protected, their numbers continue to decline.

Denmark is home in the summer months to a surprising number of butterflies, many of which migrate from the Mediterranean.

The seas around Denmark are an important breeding ground for fish, with abundant cod, herring, and plaice. The waters are also rich in sea mammals, including dolphins, porpoises, and seals.

FOUR SEASONS

Denmark has four distinct seasons, which many Danes feel contribute to the beauty of their country. Spring starts in March and lasts to May. In early May, the beech tree, the national tree of Denmark, comes into leaf.

Summer has temperatures of 78 to 88°F (27 to 33°C) on the hottest days. Summer also brings 17.5 hours of daylight. It does not get dark until after 10 P.M. Indeed, at the height of summer the night sky never seems to get completely dark. The summer months are also the wettest, and several days in a row might bring gray skies and rain.

The first signs of autumn appear around September; by October the forests are brown, as trees shed their leaves in preparation for the coming winter. In a typical year, Denmark might receive 120 days of freezing weather. On average there are between 20 and 30 days of snow, although snowfall is not guaranteed and will certainly not be as heavy as in Norway or Sweden to the north. Indeed, the last few years have brought a spell of exceptionally mild winters. Denmark gets around seven hours of sunlight in winter, and this has a big influence on the Danish lifestyle. It is dark when people leave for work and dark when they return home.

A house with a turf roof in the Faeroe Islands.

FAEROE ISLANDS

The Faeroes are a group of islands in the North Atlantic Ocean, almost halfway between northern Europe and Iceland. They are made of volcanic rock, with peaks rising to nearly 3,000 feet (900 m). The North Atlantic Drift keeps the temperature remarkably mild for such a northerly position, but the Faeroes receive heavy rainfall and fierce storms and are often covered by a thick blanket of fog and mist. The summer months produce at least a few hot and clear days. Summer days are long and nights very short, while winter brings only a few hours of sunlight each day.

Seventeen of the 18 largest islands are inhabited, and the total population is nearly 50,000. Fishing occupies over a quarter of the workforce, so declining fish stocks have created a serious threat to the economy. The Faeroes are deeply in debt and require a heavy annual grant from the Danish government. However, recent years have seen the islands take a higher profile. Faeroe teams compete in European sporting events, and the islands have become increasingly popular with tourists.

GREENLAND

Greenland is the world's largest island. It lies 2,000 miles (600 km) north of Denmark and is surrounded by the cold North Atlantic and Arctic oceans, giving it an arctic climate. It is so cold in the interior that the snow never melts. Instead, one layer of snow is compressed into ice by the weight of subsequent snowfalls. Eighty-five percent of the island lies beneath this permanent ice cap, which is up to 5,000 feet (1,500 m) deep. Glaciers are pushed down from the ice cap into the fjords below. The Jacobshavn Glacier can move as much as 30 feet (9 m) a day.

However, rich stocks of fish, birds, and sea mammals encouraged early human hunters to brave these inhospitable conditions. Today Greenland's population is concentrated along the ice-free coastal areas of the southwest. Fishing is the main industry, with a small number of shepherds or cattle farmers in the far south. Oil and gas exploration continues, and there is some optimism that Greenland might have large reserves off its western coast. However, it will be many years before this can be exploited.

Wildflowers on the island of Skjoldungen in Greenland. Greenland is considered part of the North American continent but is politically part of Denmark.

COPENHAGEN

Copenhagen (København in Danish) is Denmark's capital city. Greater Copenhagen is home to 1.7 million people, nearly a third of the national population. Despite its size, the city remains pleasant, safe, and clean.

Copenhagen was founded around 800 years ago by Bishop Absalon. It did not become the capital until 1443, but after that, it quickly grew into the cultural and political center of the country. During the next 200 years many of the grand buildings that give the city center its special character were constructed. Over the centuries, Copenhagen has survived wars, plagues, and fires. The destructive fires of 1728 and 1795 allowed the planners to redesign the city and create many of its present-day boulevards, parks, and gardens.

By the start of this century, Copenhagen had become the center of Denmark's industrial growth, bringing new prosperity. The city is famous for its breweries and porcelain factories, but these are actually less important to the economy than the engineering, clothing, and food processing industries.

In 2002 the first part of a new metro system opened, improving communications between the city center and the suburbs. The new subway trains are fully automated and operate without a driver. Kastrup Airport, just a few miles from the city center, has grown into one of the busiest airports in Europe.

OTHER CITIES

Apart from Copenhagen, the rest of Denmark's cities have the atmosphere of small towns.

ÅRHUS Århus is the second largest city. It is located in eastern Jutland and traces its history back to a Viking settlement. Today it is an important industrial center and has the second largest university in the country, in addition to a school of journalism. Many people find the pace of life here more relaxing than in Copenhagen.

ODENSE Odense lies on the island of Fyn at the center of some of Denmark's richest farmland. Although it is a major industrial city and shipbuilding center, the city center still has many beautiful old buildings. These include the childhood home of Hans Christian Andersen, now one of Denmark's finest museums.

ÅLBORG Ålborg, in northern Jutland, is the fourth largest Danish city. A bridge across the Limford River joins it with the residential areas on the northern bank, which are now considered part of greater Ålborg. There are important brick and cement industries that use local clay and chalk, and the modern port is the main link with Greenland. The city has its own zoo and Tivoli Park.

HISTORY

THERE IS EVIDENCE that people were living in Denmark as long ago as 50,000 B.C., but these primitive hunters were driven out by the last ice age. Nomadic tribes returned with the warmer weather and resettled the area around 14,000 years ago. This was the Stone Age, when people used flint to produce high-quality tools and weapons.

The period around 1500 B.C. brought two major technological advances. Farming was transformed by the invention of the wooden plow, and people learned to make metal tools from copper and bronze. As the Danish tribes became richer, important trading links were established with the more advanced nations to the south. We know very little about the politics of the time, but the land was probably divided into small tribal areas, each ruled by a local chieftain. It was not until around A.D. 400 that larger villages appeared. These are the first signs that political power was starting to concentrate in the hands of a few individuals.

Left: **An important change occurred about 4000 B.C., when people learned to clear forests and settle in one area as farmers. These first farming communities built the large stone tombs that can still be seen in the Danish countryside.**

Opposite: **A statue of King Frederik V stands in the center of the cobblestone square of the royal palace in Copenhagen.**

Viking warriors were known for their fierceness in battle.

THE VIKING PERIOD

From the ninth to the 11th centuries, Viking warriors from Denmark and the other Scandinavian countries raided much of Europe, bringing terror wherever they sailed. The first record of a Viking raid dates to 793, when warriors attacked the English monastery of Lindisfarne. They took the little community by surprise, plundering the church and killing or carrying off the monks.

We cannot be certain what social or political changes provoked these raids, but one major factor might well have been a growth in population that left many people without sufficient farmland.

At first the Vikings made only brief raids, burning small villages and then fleeing back to the sea. However, the death of King Charlemagne of France in 814 weakened mainland Europe and allowed the Vikings to become bolder. Danish Vikings were soon sailing up the major rivers of Europe to plunder cities in England, France, and Germany. Raiding eventually gave way to conquest and by 878 a Danish Grand Army had seized a large part of eastern England. In 911 the King of France gave the province of Normandy to the Viking chieftain Rollo in return for Rollo's protection. In 1013 King Canute of Denmark subjugated all of England. Danish kings occupied the throne of England until the death of King Harthacnut in 1042, when the Viking period is considered to have ended, although Duke William the Conqueror of Normandy, who conquered England in 1066, was a direct descendent of the Viking chieftain Rollo.

LIFE IN A VIKING SOCIETY

A typical Viking home had one large building with a single room where both people and animals slept. This was made from timber and stone and had wattle and daub walls. There was very little furniture. The head of the house might have a bed and a chair, but the rest of the family slept on mats that were laid out on the floor each night. Valuables were stored in wooden chests, but most objects were hung on the walls. A fire pit in the middle of the room was used for cooking and heating.

Most Danes at this time lived on isolated farms or in small villages, but there were also a few larger settlements. Hedeby was a particularly wealthy trading town at the foot of the Jutland Peninsula. The sites of several large fortified camps have also been discovered. Ribe was a hub for Viking activity, and there is a center there that recreates the way of life of the Vikings with reconstructed sites and live re-enactments.

During the Viking period, Denmark was primarily agricultural. Vikings cultivated barley, rye, oats, and wheat. Farmers kept cattle, pigs, horses, sheep, and goats. Warriors were recruited from the farmers.

The first mention of Ribe dates from 862, when the town was a well-organized trade center where markets were held regularly.

19

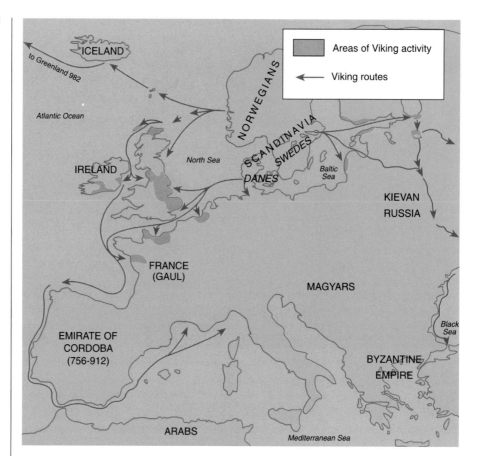

Viking ships often sailed with mixed crews, with the warriors coming from all parts of the Scandinavian region. However, evidence suggests that most of the raids on southern England were the work of Vikings from Denmark, while Norwegian Vikings played the major role in attacks on Scotland and Ireland.

EXPLORERS OF THE SEA

Sailing in their open wooden boats, the Vikings explored the coastline of Europe and navigated down the great Russian rivers. Other ships ventured west into the dangerous North Atlantic, where they colonized Iceland and Greenland. Leif Erikson and his crew sailed even farther, exploring the shores of North America in A.D. 1000.

Nordic shipbuilders designed crafts that were both light and strong. Their ships tapered at both ends and were steered by a single rudder at the stern. The ships were powered by a large, square sail, but they could also be rowed. The long ship was a battle craft carrying up to 40 warriors. It could be over 90 feet (27.4 m) in length and was low and narrow. Merchant ships, in contrast, were tall and wide and had a covered deck.

A WONDERFUL FIND

An old tradition claimed that a galleon had been sunk in the Roskilde Fjord to block one channel and protect the town of Roskilde from raids. When divers explored the sea bed, they found the remains of five ships. More importantly, the find was much older than people had expected and dated to the Viking period.

An iron enclosure was placed around the wrecks, and the water was pumped out. Hundreds of years on the sea bed had flattened the crafts, and their timber was rotten and crumbling. Over 50,000 separate pieces of wood were discovered, each of which had to be carefully dried out and preserved. The remains of the ships were reassembled piece by piece.

Two of the craft were warships, including a long ship for 40 warriors, but there were also two merchant ships and a fishing or ferry boat. Today the Roskilde ships are housed in a museum on the edge of the fjord.

The name Viking *appears on early runic stones and was always used in connection with sea battles. The fierce sailors in their long ships were also known as Norsemen, Northmen, or Danes. The Franks called them Ascomans or Normanni, and the Arabs, Rus or al-Magus.*

This bedroom in Frederiksborg Castle is decorated in the style of the 17th century.

A BALTIC POWER

Denmark had entered the Viking period as a little-known collection of tribes on the edge of Europe. It emerged three centuries later as a powerful nation, united under one king, that had extended its influence over much of the Baltic Sea region.

Valdemar I, who came to the throne in 1157, was the greatest king of this new age. With the assistance of Bishop Absalon he restored Denmark's declining military power and established schools, fortresses, churches, and monasteries throughout the country. About half the modern cities in Denmark, including Copenhagen, were founded during his reign.

Beginning in 1240 a series of weak kings conceded power to the nobles and clergy, and Denmark suffered a long period of civil war. It was over a century before Valdemar IV reunited the country. His daughter, Queen Margrethe, united Denmark, Sweden, and Norway in the Union of Kalmar in 1397. Copenhagen became the political and cultural center of the region. Sweden broke away from the union in 1523, but Norway was ruled by Denmark for the next 300 years.

The breakup of the union left Denmark and Sweden as regional rivals and led to a series of wars. The Danes lost most of their territory to the Swedes during the war of 1657–60. In 1700 they attempted to regain this lost territory, but although the Great Northern War dragged on for more than 20 years it achieved little. In the Protestant Reformation of 1536, King Christian III converted Denmark from a Catholic to a Protestant nation.

THE LOSS OF AN EMPIRE

The 18th and 19th centuries saw a new balance of power in Europe force Denmark into further conflicts. Denmark tried to stay neutral in the Napoleonic Wars, but in 1807 the British bombarded Copenhagen for war supplies and captured most of the Danish navy. Denmark then formed an alliance with France and consequently lost possession of Norway after the French defeat. In 1848 a revolution broke out in the provinces of Schleswig and Holstein. These were ruled by the Danish king but were not part of Denmark. The rebels wanted to end Danish rule and join the German Confederation. Danish troops put down the revolution, but when they tried to make Schleswig part of Denmark, Prussia intervened. In 1864 Prussian and Austrian troops invaded Denmark and after a quick victory took over both Schleswig and Holstein.

SOCIAL CHANGES

While Denmark's military power was declining, important social and economic reforms were taking place at home. The latter part of the 18th century brought the abolition of serfdom. Important land reforms that enabled farmers to buy the land they worked followed. This gave people a taste for freedom, and in 1849 King Frederick VII was forced to accept a democratic constitution that established a new parliament.

Trade and industry grew considerably in the 19th century, and farmers improved efficiency by organizing into cooperatives. Despite such progress, the end of the century saw a major economic depression. Farmers were badly hit, and many emigrated to the United States. The rest switched from growing grain to raising livestock, marking the beginning of the modern agricultural industry. In 1915 a new constitution ended the special rights of the upper class, laying the foundation for Danish democracy.

Denmark has many dairy farms, because many farmers switched from growing grain to raising livestock in the late 19th century.

WORLD WAR II AND AFTER

The decade of the 1930s was a difficult period for the country, particularly for the farmers, who were badly hit by the world depression. At the same time, Hitler's rise to power in Germany cast a threatening cloud over Europe. In 1939 Denmark signed a pact with Germany, promising neither country would attack the other. When war broke out in Europe a few months later, the Danes did not expect their country to be directly involved. However, on April 9, 1940, German troops made a surprise attack on Denmark, overcoming Danish resistance in a few hours.

At first the Danes were allowed to retain their own government, but as the war dragged on, German rule became harsher and Danish resistance stronger. Trains and factories were sabotaged, and in August 1943, the German army took over the running of the country. When the Germans attempted to deport Denmark's Jewish population, the Danes responded by hiding most of the country's Jewish families until they could be smuggled to safety in Sweden.

Denmark came out of the war with relatively little damage to its cities or industry, and the 1950s brought dramatic growth in the nation's wealth. In the postwar period Denmark strengthened its ties with the rest of Europe. Denmark became a member of the North Atlantic Treaty Organization (NATO) in 1949 and joined the European Economic Community (EEC), now the European Union (EU), in 1973. It also has strong affiliations with the Nordic Council, assuming the presidency in 2005.

Another postwar challenge was to redefine the role of former colonies. Iceland was granted independence in 1945, while the Faeroe Islands and Greenland were granted home rule in 1948 and 1979, respectively.

RECENT HISTORY

The election of 1982 resulted in a swing in politics, with Poul Schlüter becoming the first Conservative prime minister in almost a century. One of the major decisions of his government was to ban the building of nuclear power stations. By the end of the decade many Danes were becoming disenchanted with the European Union. In 1992 the country voted against ratifying the Maastricht Treaty, and in 2000 it voted to reject the euro. However, ties with the other Scandinavian countries remained as close as ever. In 2000, for example, Denmark and Sweden opened the 10-mile (16-km) Øresund Bridge to connect their two countries.

In 2001 Danish politics took a turn when a conservative coalition led by Anders Fogh Rasmussen won power. One of the key issues for the new government was the promise to tighten immigration rules.

Denmark took part in the 2001 U.S.-led invasion of Afghanistan and sent a small force of around 500 troops to Iraq in 2003. The 2004 Madrid train bombings made many Danes wonder if this policy might make their own country a target for terrorism.

Environmental concerns were a major issue during the mid-1980s. In 1987 Denmark's parliament passed very strong environmental protection laws.

GOVERNMENT

DENMARK IS A CONSTITUTIONAL MONARCHY, with the queen as chief of state. The present ruler is Queen Margrethe II. Denmark has the oldest unbroken royal line in Europe; its royal family dates to King Gorm in 930. Today, however, the prime minister is the actual head of government.

The prime minister is the leader of the majority party or, as is usually the case in Denmark, coalition of parties. One of the prime minister's most important jobs is to form the cabinet. Members of the cabinet oversee different areas of the government. They also advise the prime minister during cabinet meetings.

Parliament has a single chamber called the Folketing (folk-keh-TING). It has 179 elected members, including two from Greenland and two from the Faeroe Islands.

Every Dane over 18 is entitled to vote, and elections are held every four years. The normal turnout is over 90 percent of the eligible population.

There is proportional representation with a 2 percent limit. This means that any party gaining more than 2 percent of the total vote is guaranteed seats in parliament. The usual outcome of this system is that many different parties are represented in the Folketing, so that a majority can only be achieved if several parties join together in a coalition.

The parliament frequently uses referendums. If one-third of the members of parliament call for a referendum, that issue must be put to the population. This allows the public to vote on important or controversial decisions. In recent years, issues such as its membership within the European Union and lowering the voting age have been decided by referendum.

The current prime minister is Anders Fogh Rasmussen, who has been in power since 2001. He is a member of the Venstre (Liberal) Party and leads a coalition with the Conservatives.

The Danish flag with a white cross on a red background is the oldest national flag in the world. We know for certain that it was used by King Valdemar IV, who ruled in the middle of the 14th century. However, according to legend, it fell from the sky, as an omen for the Danish army at the Battle of Lyndanisse in 1219 during a Danish crusade in present-day Estonia.

Opposite: **Changing guards at Amalienborg Palace.**

Copenhagen Town Hall. Each county or municipality has an elected council headed by a mayor.

THE STRUCTURE OF GOVERNMENT

There are 18 ministries, including those of Justice, Finance, and Foreign Affairs. The Environment ministry was formed to deal with issues such as pollution. The Energy ministry oversees the North Sea gas and oil reserves. The Social and Cultural Affairs ministry has been reorganized as the Social Affairs ministry and the Gender Equality ministry.

Each ministry is headed by a cabinet member. Civil servants within the ministry do not change when there is a new government. They are expected to serve the government that is in power.

Denmark is divided into 14 counties and two metropolitan areas (Copenhagen and Frederiksberg). The counties are divided into over 200 municipalities, each with an elected municipal board. A reform began in 2004 to reduce the number of municipalities, bringing them under larger municipalities or regional authorities. The county authorities are responsible for major roads, hospitals, and secondary schools within their area. The municipal boards are in charge of water, gas, electricity, social welfare, primary schools, libraries, and minor roads.

THE EUROPEAN UNION

In 1973 Denmark entered the European Community. In February 1992, the Maastricht Treaty was formulated, changing the European Community to the European Union. The European Union envisages broad changes in the relationships of its members, including the evolution of a supranational federal Europe with a full monetary union, a common currency, and the removal of all trade barriers.

The Danish government sometimes seems more in favor of the European Union than the Danish people. In 1992 the Folketing voted to approve the Maastricht Treaty, but 50.7 percent of Danes voted against ratification in a referendum. The treaty was approved in a second referendum, but only after Denmark was given exemption from certain provisions, including participation in a common defense policy and a single currency. Another national referendum rejected the euro, even though once again the idea was supported by the government.

THE PARLIAMENT BUILDING

Denmark is governed from Slotsholmen Island in the center of Copenhagen. The Folketing is housed there in Christiansborg Palace, one of the most beautiful parliament buildings in the world. This grand U-shaped building with its distinctive tower was built at the turn of the century. In front is a statue of King Frederik VII, who established the modern parliament.

Most ministries are located on the island. Several, including that of Finance, are housed in the nearly 300-year-old Red Building. Recently the Ministry of Foreign Affairs decided there was no longer adequate room on Slotsholmen, and they opened additional offices in another part of the city. This is a trend that other ministries will no doubt be forced to follow in the future.

Ålborg town hall.

THE PARTIES

The Liberal Party is the major partner in the coalition government with the Conservative People's Party. The main issues for the Liberal Party are tax and immigration. The Conservative People's Party is one of Denmark's oldest and most important parties. It has often been part of a coalition government but only once—from 1982 to 1993—provided the prime minister.

With a minority of seats in parliament, the Liberal-Conservative coalition needs the support of the Danish People's Party. Together, the three parties have 95 of the 179 seats. The Danish People's Party was founded in 1995 after a group of ministers left the Progress Party. It is a nationalistic political party that is often portrayed as being "far-right," although this is moderate when compared to the Republican Party in the United States. It supports an anti-immigration policy and wants Denmark to leave the European Union. In the 2005 elections it took 24 seats making it the third largest party in Denmark.

The Social Democrats are historically the most successful party in Denmark and were traditionally supported by the trade unions. In the 2001 elections they only took 29.1 percent of the votes. This was the first time since the war they had not been Denmark's most popular party. The Radical Liberal Party, or Danish Social Liberal Party, gained seven more seats in 2005, bringing its total to 16. Much of its success is due to the popularity of its leader, Marianne Jelved, who has spoken out against the anti-immigration policy. The Socialist Party has 11 seats, and the Unity List-Red Green Alliance six seats.

MARGRETHE II, DENMARK'S QUEEN

Queen Margrethe *(above, second from left)* was born in Amalienborg Castle in 1940, just a few days after Germany invaded Denmark. Her birth gave the Danish people something to celebrate at this terrible moment in their history.

In 1953, when it was clear there would not be a male heir, new laws were passed to allow female succession. Margrethe was carefully educated in politics, economics, and history in college. In 1967 she married Count Henri de Laborde, a French diplomat, with whom she has two sons: Crown Prince Frederik, born in 1968; and Prince Joachim, who is a year younger. In 2005 Crown Prince Frederik and Crown Princess Mary gave birth to a baby boy, who is heir to the 1,000-year-old Danish throne.

Queen Margrethe came to the throne in 1972 at the age of 31. She has used her influence as queen, particularly in her annual New Year's Eve address, to encourage her people to improve themselves. In 1987 she criticized her listeners for their lack of initiative: "This attitude is very familiar: it's a don't-get-too-uppity attitude, don't get too big for your boots—keep your head down, nobody will notice you. It's perhaps not untypical of village life anywhere, but in Denmark it spills over from village life into the whole country." She remains outspoken and recently approved the publication of a biography in which she speaks out against radical Islam.

The queen has considerable artistic talent. She designed sets and costumes for a television adaptation of a Hans Christian Andersen story, illustrated Tolkien's *Lord of the Rings*, translated French and Swedish novels into Danish, and designed Danish postal stamps.

ECONOMY

DENMARK IS ONE of the richest nations in the world, and Danes enjoy a high standard of living. By 2005 unemployment was at a low of 5.9 percent, and the 2005 elections suggest that many Danes are happy with the way the economy is being managed. The Danish economy is largely based on manufacturing high-quality products. Much of what Denmark produces is exported, and Queen Margrethe herself once pointed out that Danish success is based not only on their skill in making things, but also on their ability to sell them. Because exporting is so essential to the economy, it is hoped that membership in the European Union will both protect existing markets and open new opportunities.

What makes this success so remarkable is that it has been achieved despite Denmark's extremely limited mineral resources. Denmark has to

Left: **The government has started a number of programs to support the forming of small businesses.**

Opposite: **In Copenhagen, stands display flowers and produce for sale.**

import petroleum, fuels, machinery, transportation equipment, metals, and paper products. More than 80 percent of its exports consist of manufactured products such as machinery and instruments, while the remaining exports include agricultural products, fish, and fish products.

FARMING AND FISHING

Although farming has become less central to the economy in recent years, 65 percent of the land is still used for agriculture, and Denmark produces three times its own food requirements. In addition, an important part of Danish industry is linked to agriculture and processing and packaging meats, dairy products, and fish.

Danish farming is based on small family farms. Part-time labor might be employed at busy times, but statistics show that only one in six farms employ full-time help. Ninety percent of the agricultural income comes from animal products. Principal activities are pig and dairy farming. Because of the large numbers of animals in Denmark, much of the grain and vegetables

harvested are used as animal feed. Barley is the most common crop and takes up around half of all Danish farmland. Danish ham, bacon, and butter are particularly popular in Britain and Germany.

In recent years rising costs have made life difficult for small farmers, and the number of farms has fallen from 200,000 to less than 100,000. Those that have continued have often had to search for alternative sources of income, such as taking in tourists or renting out buildings. In 1989 legislation permitted the formation of larger farms, indicating a change in the traditional government protection of family farms.

Fishing has been important to the Danish economy for hundreds of years, but since the 1980s the industry has been going through a crisis, due largely to overfishing. By 2001 there were only 2,500 full-time registered fishermen left in Denmark and the government had been paying grants to help take boats out of service.

However, Denmark is still one of the world's major fishing nations; in 2003 its fish exports were worth $2.8 billion and accounted for about 3.5 percent of its exports. There is also an important supporting industry

Almost all captains own their boats, and even the larger deepsea ships tend to be run by small companies that maintain just one or two vessels. The income from each trip is usually divided, half going to meet the cost of the boat, the rest being divided up among the crew.

involving the canning and freezing of fish. This industry has to buy much of its fish from outside of Denmark.

INDUSTRY

Among the most important Danish industrial products are electrical goods, ceramics, medical goods, textiles, and toys.

Danish industry prides itself on adapting to market demands. For example, Denmark's experience in making electrical goods has been transferred to the new growth area of high-technology computer equipment. Some of the most successful Danish computer firms are those that specialize in developing computer software for use in industry.

A LAND OF SCIENCE

Denmark has produced many great scientists who have played an important part in developing Danish industry as well as advancing human knowledge. The most famous Danish scientist of this century is Nobel Prize winner Niels Bohr *(left)*, one of the founders of modern nuclear physics. His son, Aage Bohr, took up his work and also won the Nobel Prize. In the field of physics, H.C. Ørsted discovered electromagnetism, while Ole Romer first approximated the speed of light.

Other notable scientists include Johannes Fibiger, who did pioneer work on treating cancer, Valdemar Poulsen, who helped invent the modern tape recorder, and Henrik Dam, who discovered vitamin K. Danish scientists are particularly respected for their work in medical and technological research.

Much of Danish industry is small- or medium-sized, with a typical firm employing a hundred people or less. The biggest companies in Denmark include: the transportation firm Moller-Maersk; the TDC Group, which provides telecommunications services; Novo-Nordisk, which makes drugs and biotechnology; and Carlsberg, which makes food, drink, and tobacco products. One of the most successful stories has been wind technology, and 60 percent of all the wind turbines used around the world have been made in Denmark.

A LACK OF NATURAL RESOURCES

Denmark has extremely limited mineral resources. There are deposits of limestone, clay, gravel, granite, and kaolin (a white clay used to manufacture porcelain), but Denmark stills needs to import all of its raw metals and coal, and until recently all of its oil. Fortunately, offshore oil fields in the North Sea have been producing petroleum since 1972 and natural gas since 1984.

There is optimism that Denmark will develop pollution-free energy sources in the future. In 1980 Denmark decided not to develop nuclear energy. Danish engineers are experimenting with other energy schemes.

BLACK GOLD

Denmark's share of the North Sea oil fields produce about 332,100 barrels of oil a day. This is more than Denmark uses, so there is a surplus for export. However, because there are different types of oil, Denmark still has to buy some of its oil from other countries. It is uncertain how long the North Sea reserves will last. The prediction is that technology has enabled the oil fields to be exploited quicker than was expected and that the point of peak production has already been passed.

Tax rates in Denmark are very high, at around 50 percent for income tax and 25 percent for sales tax. As a result, "moonlighting," which means taking on private work without declaring the income to the government, is very common.

Future domestic energy needs may be met with biogas produced from industrial waste, bleached earth, and cattle manure.

The strong winds blowing in from the sea have enormous potential, and there are already hundreds of wind turbines scattered through the Danish countryside. This has been a major success, and wind energy is providing about 10 percent of the nation's power requirements. Some people predict that by 2030 half the country's electricity could be coming from 'turbine parks.'

WORKING

Forty years ago nearly one in three Danes was employed in agriculture, and even 20 years ago food products were still Denmark's top export. Today agriculture employs only 3 percent of the workforce. Instead, industry and public service employ half of all Danes. Most Danes feel that they work hard, and much of the nation's success is indeed due to the well-educated and highly skilled workforce. This work ethic is established during childhood when Danish children are encouraged to find afterschool jobs, such as delivering newspapers or leaflets.

At the same time, it is very much part of Danish culture that work should not be allowed to dominate life. The standard work week is only 37 hours, and 75 percent of Danish people work a five-day week.

The unemployment rate in Denmark has been falling since 1994. Once over 12 percent, it now hovers around 6 percent. However, there are areas of concern. Immigrants, especially those from outside Europe or North America, have had trouble fitting into the system and experience much higher rates of unemployment. Furthermore, in the long term, Danes have to face up to the problem of a smaller workforce supporting a larger population of retired people.

TRANSPORTATION

The Danish transportation system is modern and efficient and can usually cope with even the worst of Danish winters. Cycling is a popular mode of transportation on land. Interconnected national, regional, and local bicycle routes make it easy for people to go almost anywhere in the country by bicycle.

Being an island nation has posed its own special problems, and Danish engineers are now some of the most experienced bridge builders in the world. A bridge and tunnel combination that spans the Great Belt to link the islands of Zealand and Fyn opened in 1999. The Øresund Bridge makes it possible to travel from Copenhagen to the Swedish city of Malmö in just 20 minutes. In addition, ferries continue to play an important role in linking many of the islands and in connecting Denmark with Sweden and Norway.

Denmark, Norway, and Sweden run a combined airline called Scandinavian Airlines System (SAS). It is one of the largest airlines in Europe, with a reputation for good service. However, like many national airlines, it is struggling to compete with budget airlines.

Shipping is an important activity at Skagen in north Jutland.

SHIPPING AND TRADE

Denmark's shipbuilding tradition stretches back to the Viking period, but just a few years ago the industry appeared to be on the point of collapse. Denmark's share of global shipbuilding had fallen to just 1 percent, with most of the trade going to South Korea, and several important shipyards had closed down. The Danish shipbuilding industry fought back by making a large investment in robot technology, while at the same time marketing the Danish reputation for outstanding engineering.

In 2005 the Odense Steel Shipyard launched a giant container ship, the first major Danish-built ship for several years. The shipyard is busy again, and there is hope that the industry might bounce back. Denmark also maintains a large merchant fleet. Danish shipping companies have a reputation for high standards and safety, and with more ships on order the fleet is expected to expand over the next few years.

LEGO—ONE OF THE WORLD'S GREAT TOYS

Lego, from the words *leg godt,* meaning "play well," is one of Denmark's most famous exports. At the Legoland amusement park *(below)* everything is made of Legos. These interlocking toy building bricks are popular with children throughout the world. In fact, Lego is such a universally recognized name that many people do not even realize that it is a Danish invention.

The Lego empire was started in the 1930s by a carpenter called Ole Kirk Christiansen. During the depression there were few customers for his furniture, so Christiansen started to make sets of toy bricks out of wood. After World War II, he set up a factory to mass-produce his bricks from plastic, and they soon became one of the most popular toys in the world. It seems typical of the Danes to take an educational toy and make it such an outstanding commercial success.

ENVIRONMENT

DENMARK WAS THE FIRST country in the world to establish a ministry for the environment. The nation has also signed many international environmental agreements, such as the Antarctic Treaty and others on a variety of issues including biodiversity, endangered species, whaling, pollution, ozone depletion, climate change, desertification, wetlands conservation, and hazardous waste. There are hundreds of environmental projects going on around the country, and Danes are also helping with environmental projects in other countries, such as Malaysia, Cambodia, and South Africa.

However, Denmark is a small country that has been farmed for many years. Much of the original forest has been lost. In fact about 95 percent of the land surface has been modified in some way. In addition, Denmark lies at the center of industrial Europe, and the Danish environment is affected by what their neighbors do. The Danish Ministry of the Environment has

Left: **Turbines on a wind farm in Fyn generate electricity without the pollution that results in the production of energy from burning fossil fuels.**

Opposite: **A tree-lined road near Haslev in Roskilde.**

Opposite: **The antlers of the red deer stag have for centuries made Denmark's largest mammal a target of human hunters.**

Below: **A river flows by a house in Jutland. Jutland's rivers are the last natural habitat for the endangered houting. There have been initiatives to make the region's rivers more accessible to spawning houting.**

therefore been providing environmental assistance to countries from the former USSR, which are responsible for much of the pollution in the Baltic Sea. The Danish government's goal is to have an unpolluted sea and a 21-percent reduction of emissions of greenhouse gases by 2020.

CLEANER WATER, CLEANER AIR

A great deal of effort has gone into cleaning Denmark's water, and only 5 miles (8 km) of the nation's 3,000 miles (4,828 km) of beaches are now considered unsafe for swimming. Modern water purification plants not only take out organic matter, but also remove nitrogen and phosphorus.

As a result, many rivers are much cleaner than they were a few years ago and are once again well stocked with fish. However, lakes and inlets, where the water does not get exchanged so quickly, have proved more difficult to deal with. A major problem is that the nitrate-nitrogen used in fertilizers runs off the farmer's fields and collects in the water. Farming can also cause pollution with ammonia, which comes from piggeries and pig manure.

Since 1997, the air in Danish cities has become notably cleaner. The conversion to unleaded gasoline has been a particular success. However, traffic remains a major cause of air pollution. Denmark is also phasing out the use of dangerous chemicals that destroy the ozone layer.

RETURNING WILDLIFE

The largest animal found in Denmark is the red deer. There are also roe and fallow deer, and smaller animals such as hares, foxes, squirrels, and badgers.

Denmark is an important resting place for many migrating birds. The country is trying to create more areas where wildlife can live, and some rivers that had been straightened are once again being allowed to follow their natural courses and to overflow their banks.

The deciduous forest in Lystrup is home to the ring-necked pheasant, whose natural habitat includes woodlands, grasslands, and farmland.

This creates wet meadows, which are wonderful for birds and also help prevent flooding. The Skjern River Nature Project has won international environmental awards for turning 5,500 acres (2,225 hectares) of cultivated land back into wetland.

Where woodlands have been left untouched, beech and oak are likely to be the most common trees, but you might also find trees such as elm, hazel, maple, pine, birch, and chestnut. Many of the woods that have survived were once royal hunting areas. Some new forests are also being planted and the plan is to double the country's woodland area over the next 80 years.

Hunting is now better controlled, allowing the roe deer numbers to increase. Otter numbers are slowly increasing in Jutland and beavers have been reintroduced. Some rare birds such as the spoonbill and the peregrine falcon are also increasing in numbers, and in 2004 gray seals started breeding in Danish waters again.

A few animals have successfully adapted to living close to people, and they can be found in large numbers on the edges of Danish towns. These include foxes and hedgehogs as well as birds such as sparrows, blackbirds, and starlings.

PROGRESS IN THE HOME

Denmark has put considerable effort into the problem of waste disposal. The first plan is to recycle as much as possible. Rubbish that cannot be recycled is incinerated, with the energy produced being used for heating.

A warning sign for cyclists in Copenhagen. For Danes, cycling is the preferred mode of transportation not only for economic but also environmental reasons.

BIRD WATCHING FOR THE EXPERTS

Danish bird life is particularly rich with 400 different species, and bird watching is very popular in Denmark. One does not have to leave the capital to catch glimpses of bird activity—the city parks are home to many kinds of birds *(below, geese at the Frilandsmuseet open-air museum in Copenhagen)*. However, Danish bird watchers would be particularly excited to see any of these:

- Cranes: Only a dozen or so pairs breed in Denmark.
- Spoonbills: There is a small colony in northern Jutland.
- White storks: This bird is nearly extinct in Denmark. In 2000 there were probably only three breeding pairs.
- White-tailed eagles: This bird recently returned to Denmark, where it was last observed breeding in 1912.
- Eagle owls: This bird returned to Denmark in recent years.
- Black grouses: This bird is nearly extinct but a few are spotted each year.
- Golden eagles: One pair has been seen breeding in Denmark in recent years.

Rubbish is dumped only as a last resort, and there are heavy duties to discourage this. Denmark produced 12.8 million tons of waste in 2003, compared to 13.1 million tons in 2002. The industry sector reduced waste production by as much as 20 percent.

Denmark also uses several systems of labeling to allow people to buy eco-friendly products. 'The Flower' is a European Union symbol to show environmentally friendly products, while 'The Swan' is a similar system operated by the Nordic Council. Denmark also has an "Ø" label to show organically produced goods.

WILDLIFE STILL IN DANGER

Despite all these efforts there are still problems, particularly with the loss of ponds and forests. As a result, the Red Book of endangered species lists 89 Danish animals. These include everything from tiny beetles and insects to whales. The declining number of frogs and other amphibians is an area of major concern. This is partly due to the loss of breeding ponds. Not only are there fewer places for frogs to breed, but the ponds have also become farther apart.

There are about 1,000 species of plants that are indigenous to Denmark and another 200 or so species that have been introduced and are now established in the country. Many indigenous plants are declining in number, with farming being the main cause. In the last hundred years better methods of drainage and fertilization have enabled farming to take over more marginal land, decreasing the number of wild plants.

A rhinoceros calf sniffs a carrot in the Givskud Zoo in Jutland. The birth of this calf in 2005 was the first in Denmark in two decades.

DANES

THE DANES ARE A GROUP of Nordic Scandinavians who have mixed relatively little with other ethnic groups. For this reason, tall people with blond hair and blue eyes tend to predominate, although Danes display a range of heights and hair colors. There are about 5.4 million Danes living in their homeland. They also form the majority of people in Greenland and the Faeroe Islands. In addition, there are large communities of Danes living around the world, including about 400,000 people of Danish descent in the United States.

Above: **Danes are still attached to their Viking roots. These street musicians in Copenhagen are dressed in fanciful Viking costumes.**

Opposite: **Danes at the Roskilde summer rock festival.**

A summary of the Danish character might include descriptions such as friendly, sociable, and talkative. The Danes have been described as "nice and friendly, if a little boring," although American writer Evelyn Waugh called them "the most exhilarating people in the world." By Swedish and Norwegian standards, Danes are relaxed and bohemian, but their social life retains some elements of formality by North American standards. They are perhaps best described as a middle-of-the-road, middle-class society. This is a result of the tradition of *Janteloven* (YEN-tell-oh-en), where people are taught to keep a low profile, not to seek or gain attention by having different ideas, and definitely not to stand out in a crowd.

At the same time, Danes dislike restrictive legislation. They have a tradition of questioning authority, supporting the underdog, and having equal human rights for all. Hans Christian Andersen's fairy tales are typical of the Danish humanitarian tradition: the ugly duckling becomes the swan, and the vain emperor turns out to be naked.

*Danes have great
concern for the
environment.
Public support
has enabled
the government
to pass tough
environmental
laws. Danes have
become some of
the world's best
recyclers.*

FREEDOM AND RESPONSIBILITY

Danish people take the concept of personal freedom extremely seriously. Their country has one of the lowest crime rates in Europe, but they can be stubborn about obeying minor rules. Danish drivers seldom seem to take the speed limits seriously. Nor will the average law-abiding Dane think twice about bringing in extra alcohol and cigarettes when they come back from a vacation.

The basic belief in freedom makes Danish society tolerant toward personal relationships. People can be seen exchanging signs of affection on the street, holding hands or kissing, in a way that would bring disapproval in Europe's more conservative cultures. Swedes are often critical of Danish behavior, and "it wouldn't happen here" is one of their favorite expressions when talking about their neighbors.

Another important characteristic of the Danish people is their concern for the world around them. Denmark is one of the few nations meeting the United Nations' target of donating 1 percent of its gross national product to third-world countries. In addition, Denmark donates large amounts of money from individuals during international disasters.

A NUMBER FOR LIFE

Every Danish person has an identity number, known as a personal number. This is used in all dealings with the government. In banks or offices a person is often asked their number before, or even instead of, their name. This rather impersonal approach seems strangely out of character to the way Danes normally act.

Personal numbers are made up of 10 digits. The first six numbers give the person's date of birth. The next four are random, but the last number identifies whether the person is female (even) or male (odd).

CHRISTIANIA

When the army closed down their base at Christiania in the early 1970s, a group of young people took over the old walled compound to establish a cooperative society. In 1981 the community was officially recognized as a "social experiment."

Today about a thousand people live in Christiania. Many of them are artists or those seeking a different lifestyle. They go without heating, hot water, or even a private room in return for the comradeship and freedom of the community. The buildings are run down and in need of repair, but the walls are covered with beautiful murals, and it is certainly the only area in Copenhagen where chickens run about freely in the streets!

However, the police find it difficult to patrol the area, and other Scandinavian governments have urged Denmark to close down Christiania, which they believe is a haven for regional criminals and drug dealers. In recent years Christiania has become a lot more "respectable," and on Sundays many tourists will come here to wander around. Some residents have opened coffee bars or stalls to sell handmade products. But Christiania is still not quite like the rest of the city, and there are some unique rules that tourists should beware of. For example, cameras are not allowed on some streets.

CLOTHING

Clothing in Denmark today differs very little from what you would find throughout the Western world. A lot of clothing is made in Denmark, and exclusive Danish designs sell well overseas. Blue denim is extremely popular and could even be considered the national dress of the young generation.

There is growing interest in traditional Danish clothing. For women this is a long dress with puffy sleeves worn over a white blouse. The shoulders and arms are covered, and the dresses are worn with several layers of petticoats.

Traditionally these dresses are woven at home from wool or flax. An apron in a bright checkered pattern, heavy black shoes, and a bonnet or scarf complete the outfit. There are some regional differences in bonnets, with those from Zealand being the most distinctive due to their gold and silver embroidery.

The traditional costume for men is a long jacket with coat-tails, worn unbuttoned to show off a fancy vest beneath. Trousers consist of three-quarter-length knee breeches tucked into long white socks. The shoes are made from shiny black leather with a fancy buckle, and a top hat completes the picture.

Traditional outfits might be owned by folk dancers or people going overseas who want a souvenir of their home.

Other people consider their roots to go farther back, and many families have Viking outfits ready for the Viking festivals that are staged each summer. The outfit might include the famous double-horned helmet, although this is not historically accurate, as there is no evidence that the Vikings ever wore such a headpiece.

The military have their own traditional uniforms, worn by the palace royal guard. The smart red uniforms, with their shining white cross belts and enormous bearskin hats, are brought out for ceremonial occasions.

Opposite: **Danish teenagers prefer casual clothing, especially denim pants and jackets.**

Below: **An Ålborg folkdance group displays traditional Danish dress.**

GREENLANDERS

There are about 45,000 Inuit living in Greenland. The ancestors of the Inuit emigrated there around a thousand years ago, and they consider themselves the rightful owners of the land they know as Kalaallit Nunaat.

In appearance, language, and culture, they have closer ties with the other Inuit people of Canada, Alaska, and Siberia than they do with the Danes. However, because of the long historic links with Denmark, there have been numerous intermarriages, and most Greenlanders can find Danish relations somewhere in their family tree. The main exceptions are communities in the east and far north, who live in greater isolation.

Traditionally the Inuit lifestyle was based on hunting sea mammals, which provided both food and furs. Hunting still plays a role in today's lifestyle, particularly in the more remote communities. The International Whaling Commission acknowledges the importance of the traditional hunting culture and allows Greenlanders to take a small number of fin and minke whales each year. The Greenland government divides this quota between villages. The whale meat is either used by that community or sold within Greenland.

Many Greenlanders are angry that campaigns by environmental groups have destroyed the market for seal furs. They argue that the Greenland seals are not endangered and that sealing is the only economic activity available to some isolated communities. Today it is largely the older people who make a living from small-scale hunting and fishing. They still use dogsleds, although the traditional kayak has largely been replaced by modern boats. Young Greenlanders are likely to seek work in one of the shrimp or fish processing factories or to go off to a university in Denmark.

Opposite: **The traditional dress of Greenlanders provides protection against the cold.**

Like many traditional societies, the Inuit face problems adapting to a changing world. Unemployment and alcoholism—one aggravating the other—are major concerns. Drug addiction also means that Greenland has high HIV infection rates compared with the rest of Western Europe. People are starting to realize how important it is for the Inuit to have pride in their culture, so many towns have established museums to preserve the memory of the old lifestyle.

There is also an active campaign to save the Greenlandic language. Danish is the common language of business, education, and administration, but local newspapers and radio use both Danish and Greenlandic. There are a growing number of books published in Greenlandic, and television programs are increasingly being broadcast with Greenlandic subtitles.

FAEROESE

The Faeroe Islanders also have the automatic right to live and work in Denmark. It is an offer that few people from this close-knit community have taken, although many Faeroese go to Denmark to study.

The Faeroese descended from Norwegian settlers who replaced an Irish settlement in 800. For several hundred years, the Faeroes were part of Norway. When the union between Norway and Denmark ended in 1814, the Faeroe Islands remained with Denmark. In 1948, after much debate about independence from Denmark, the Faeroes were granted home rule.

Today the population is around 47,000, distributed in settlements varying widely in size. There are about 100 towns and villages, of which the largest is Tórshavn with 16,500 inhabitants. The two smallest islands have only a single family each. More than one-third of the population resides on Streymoy, the main island.

Houses are made of wood, with a deep basement in concrete and a metal roof, although the traditional turf roof is also returning to favor. In

The Faeroese, descendents of Norwegian settlers, have features similar to Danes.

the villages, family and friends may help a young person build his or her own house. Homes in Tórshavn are expensive.

A third of the Faeroe Islands workforce make their living from fishing or fish processing. It was once believed that fish farming would have a major impact on the economy, but the industry has had problems, and there are now only about 20 fish farms left, down from a peak of 60 farms some 15 years ago. Since the land is rugged, only 6 percent is under cultivation, while the rest is used for grazing sheep.

Although unemployment is low, the choice of jobs is limited, and workers must be flexible in both trade and location.

Wages are higher at sea than on land, but fishermen have a working day of 12 to 18 hours seven days a week, and their work is physically demanding as well as dangerous. If they fish in remote areas, they may be away from home for up to five months at a time.

Faeroe Islanders are extremely proud of their history and culture. They have a rich legacy of storytelling and folk songs, and these tiny islands continue to produce award-winning writers. Another important part of the cultural heritage of the Faeroese are the folk dances and the music that accompanies these dances. These are mostly chain dances where partners are exchanged around the circle.

THE GERMAN MINORITY

In southern Jutland there is a small minority of between 15,000 and 20,000 people who can trace their origins back to Germany. In fact, this area was once part of the German duchy of Schleswig, and some of the people here might still refer to it as Nordschleswig (North Schleswig). This community has lived in Denmark for many generations, and they mix in with a much larger Danish population without any tensions or

In the late 1990s the economy was doing well, and there were hopes of finding oil offshore. This made many Faeroese think about seeking full independence. However, Danish Prime Minister Poul Nyrup Rasmussen warned that Danish grants would be phased out within four years if the island voted to become independent, and the planned referendum was never held.

THE DANISH SENSE OF HUMOR

Danes pride themselves on their sense of humor and are always willing to laugh and joke with one another. A great deal of Danish humor involves people laughing at their own mistakes and characteristics.

New Year's Eve and the first day of April are two days when playing practical jokes becomes almost a national sport. Even the major newspapers join in with the April Fool's Day fun, and there is usually some front page story reporting on a fictitious event.

A popular form of humor, particularly at summer festivals, consists of live cabaret shows that parody famous people. Politicians are frequent targets, but even the royal family is not exempt. The same kind of humor is also featured in magazines and on television.

problems. Most of this minority group can speak German but are much more likely to use Danish in everyday interactions, speaking with the regional Sønderjysk (South Jutland) dialect.

However, the German minority is determined to keep their own culture alive, and this shows in festivals such as the German autumn "lantern evening" when children parade through the streets, holding lanterns and singing traditional songs. Some of the larger towns have schools offering lessons taught in German, and German churches tend to attract larger congregations than their Danish counterparts. There is also a German minority political party, called the Schleswigsche Partei. Nevertheless, many differences, such as noticeable preferences in food, have tended to dissolve over the years.

People of Danish background living within the German-influenced areas are often more openly patriotic than other Danes. The most obvious sign is the number of Danish flags flying in gardens. Their neighbors are unable to respond to such displays, as it is illegal to fly the German flag on Danish soil.

NEW IMMIGRANTS

Until recently Denmark has been a largely homogenous country, with few new arrivals. However, somewhere between 5 and 6.8 percent of the population today are immigrants or the immediate descendants of immigrants. Immigration is certainly a controversial subject in Denmark at the moment.

Immigration largely took place in two waves. In the 1970s people were encouraged to come to Denmark as there was a lack of workers. Many of these new arrivals came from Turkey and Pakistan. In the 1990s immigration was more a result of political problems in other parts of the world, and many of this wave of immigrants came from Iran, Sri Lanka, various African nations, and the former Yugoslavia. Some of these groups tend to be very different from the Danes in culture and appearance, and this has often made it difficult for them to integrate into Danish society. The immigrant population has also tended to concentrate in cities, particularly in the Copenhagen area.

Although many of the new arrivals have been successful, particularly in opening small- and medium-sized businesses, unemployment is generally higher among immigrants. This has made some people worry about how much of a burden increased immigration will place on the social security system. Sections of the press have stirred up these fears. One paper ran a story claiming that the country's 11,000 Somali immigrants, a group that has had trouble integrating, were sending millions of dollars of social security money back to Africa each year.

The Muslim minority has received particular attention, and there are areas, such as arranged marriages, where the two cultures clash. In another example the Supreme Court ruled that a young Muslim woman could be fired from her job in a supermarket for wearing a headscarf to work.

Other European countries have been surprised at Denmark's harsh attitude. A Swedish paper published the headline "Are you all racists in Denmark?" Of course it must be pointed out that not all Danes share the same view. Although the government was re-elected on the promise of a tough immigration policy, the Danish Social Liberal Party, which takes the opposite view, also did well in the election, winning the votes of many young Danes.

LIFESTYLE

THE DANISH PEOPLE enjoy one of the highest standards of living in the world, and the strong state welfare system is a major influence on the Danish lifestyle.

Denmark was one of the first countries to introduce state social welfare schemes. Health care and education are available to all Danish people free of charge. There are generous unemployment benefits and retraining programs for those who are out of work. If Danes are sick, the government pays them 90 percent of their weekly wage. When people retire, they collect a state pension, and social services and nursing homes are available.

Whatever their income, all Danish families receive a yearly "children's check" of between $1,500 to $2,000 for each child under 18 in the family, depending on the child's age. Special allowances in the form of benefits are also given to single parents or children who have lost both parents. Parents of twins and adopted children may also receive grants.

Infant mortality has fallen to around 4 deaths in every 1,000 births, one of the best figures in the world. (The United States has a rate of 6.5 deaths in every 1,000 births.) The life expectancy is 77.4 years (the same as the United States).

Providing such services is expensive, and the *Guiness Book of Records* claims that Denmark has the highest tax rate in the world. Tax is certainly an important political issue. Some people are also worried that the high standard of the Danish social services is starting to drop. There are concerns that Danish schools are not doing as well as they once did, and people complain that they have to wait longer for treatment in hospitals. Denmark must also confront the problem of how the shrinking workforce can continue to support the growing number of elderly people.

Opposite: **Danes enjoy a coffee shop in Stroget, Copenhagen.**

Bicycling is a favorite summer activity.

TWO DIFFERENT LIFESTYLES

The weather is probably the single major influence on the Danish lifestyle, and it sometimes seems that the whole nation changes character with the seasons.

In summer, Danes take every opportunity to be outdoors in the sunshine. Favorite activities include walking, cycling, jogging, or sailing. Other people are content just to head for the nearest park to sit and relax. With the warm weather visitors flock to the popular Tivoli Gardens in Copenhagen, tour boats cruise the waterways, and restaurants start putting their tables outside on the pavement

During the summer months every small town promotes weekly festivals and outdoor concerts. Providing it does not rain, such events usually attract hundreds of spectators.

With the arrival of the cold, dark winter, social life moves indoors. People rush away from work to seek the warmth and comfort of their homes, and evenings are spent enjoying leisurely meals with friends and relatives. It is the season to create that important feeling of warmth and coziness called *hygge* (HOO-gah). For most Danes the key elements of *hygge* are usually good friends, excellent food and drink, candlelight, and an open fire.

Winter also has its own fashion. Danish cardigans are expensive and extremely popular. Because of sympathy toward the Greenlandic hunters, there has not been as strong an anti-fur movement as in other places, so fur clothing is fairly common.

RURAL AND URBAN LIFE

Although 85 percent of the population live in cities, even urban Danes
retain their love of the land. Many urban residents go to rural cottages for
summer vacations. Ten out of every 100 have a second holiday cottage
in the countryside. "Colony gardens" are also popular; these are rented
plots of land near the city where people can grow flowers, fruit, and
vegetables or maintain a small greenhouse. City dwellers often use them
for weekend retreats.

Probably the main difference between rural and urban Danes is the
close sense of community that has survived in many villages. In the village
community, people are far more likely to know their neighbors by name,
they seem to have more time to stop and talk when they meet in the
street, and they are more likely to be there to help out when somebody
has problems. City dwellers live a more hectic life.

BIRTH

Virtually all the new ideas and theories about giving birth have been published in Denmark, and each has won its share of converts. Probably the most important trend has been the growing number of Danish fathers now present at the birth of their children.

For several years the birth rate in Denmark was low, and people were predicting the population would begin to decline. Instead, the 1990s brought a slight reversal of this trend, although most families today only have one or two children.

During the development of the modern healthcare program, most births took place in hospitals. This pattern is now being reversed, with a growing number of women electing to have their babies at home, with a doctor or midwife in attendance.

This is more for economic than social reasons. Four or five days in a hospital were once quite normal after giving birth. Now the healthcare system is starting to cut costs, and most mothers are sent home within 24 hours of the birth. As a result, women seem less enthusiastic about going to the hospital.

After the birth it is usual for the mother to be given flowers, and friends and relatives bring gifts for the baby. It is highly unusual to give gifts before the baby is born. The old practice of blue gifts for boys and pink for girls also seems to be returning to fashion.

Danes believe it is very important for new families to have time together. Pregnant women have the right to four weeks free from work prior to giving birth. If there are any complications they can get a medical certificate to take a longer period of absence.

After the birth the mother must take two weeks off and is entitled to up to 14 weeks of maternity leave. The father is also entitled to two weeks of paternity leave during this period. Then, after the child is 14 weeks old, the parents can share another 32 weeks of leave. In all, a family will get 52 weeks of leave during which they will receive financial support.

BIRTHDAYS AND GROWING UP

Danes make a fuss about birthdays. On the morning of their birthday, people are expected to stay in bed. Sometime before breakfast, the family will burst in with presents and cards. They are likely to hold small Danish flags and sing the two popular Danish birthday songs. The more famous one describes events that will happen on the day. If it is a school day, children might bring cake and cookies for their classmates.

It is usual for children to have a birthday party. Guests are treated to special foods, including a cake-man, which is a cake baked in the shape of a man. Hot chocolate is another favorite on these occasions. Children also play party games, such as Pin-the-Tail-on-the-Donkey.

The 18th birthday is considered the start of adulthood. This is the age when young people can vote and drive cars. It is usual to celebrate the day with a big party. When boys pass the age of 18, they may have to

Denmark has invested a great deal of money in its school system and the standards are generally very high. Materials are plentiful and the number of children in each class is often as low as 20.

complete four to twelve months of national service in the armed forces and periodic reservist training after that. Not all Danes are called up, and a lottery determines who will have to go. Young Danes who object to military training may choose non-military positions or aid work in developing countries.

EDUCATION

School is compulsory in Denmark from the ages of 7 to 16 years. Many children also spend a year in preschool. Although there are private schools, the majority of Danish children attend the government-run *folkeskole* (FOLK-es-skoh-la). These schools combine elementary and junior high school education in one building.

Danish schools operate in pupil groups, with the same classmates staying together throughout their school life. Each pupil group is assigned to a teacher who stays with them throughout their time at the *folkeskole*. As the children become older, they have lessons with other teachers, but they still retain close contact with their original teacher.

ADULT EDUCATION

Denmark has led the way for the rest of the world in the area of adult education. Adult education is considered an important part of Danish culture, and many Danes continue their studies with evening classes or summer courses.

These courses are organized by the local authorities, which provide financial support and make school buildings available during the evenings. Subjects offered might be educational, such as history or foreign languages; recreational, such as art or photography; or vocational, such as computer studies or automobile repair.

N.F.S. Grundtvig founded the first folk high school in 1844. His idea of offering further education to adults for their personal development has been copied in the United States, England, and Canada. There are now about 80 folk high schools in Denmark, all of them residential. Courses are often sponsored by educational and commercial organizations in order to provide training or to generate interest in a particular field, especially arts or social science subjects. Those who attend courses may be following a particular interest or laying the foundation for a change of jobs.

It is common for pupils to address teachers by their first names, and the relationship is often close enough for children to phone the teacher at home when they have problems. In addition to parents coming to school for open days, schools are experimenting with teachers making visits to the children's homes so they can learn more about the family.

After the ninth grade, when the children are 15, they take a final assessment test called the leaving examination. Those who do well on this exam usually elect to go to a gymnasium, a three-year secondary school that prepares students for university study. Those who are not ready to go to a gymnasium after the ninth grade might stay in school for an extra year and take a second exam, the advanced leaving examination. There is still the chance of going to a gymnasium at the end of the 10th year. Other students typically enter a technical school or commercial school.

There are five universities in Denmark. Copenhagen University was founded in 1479. It has about 33,000 students and a teaching staff of 4,800. Århus University provides education for about 14,000 students and has about 800 full-time teachers and many part-time teachers. Odense University provides education not only in traditional academic subjects but also in music, business, social studies, and teacher training. In addition, there are numerous technical colleges and specialized training institutions.

THE ROLE OF WOMEN

Women make up a large part of the Danish workforce. Statistics show that for every 100 working men there are 86 working women. This high percentage has been possible thanks to the state-supported system of childcare. In 1990, 71 percent of children between the ages of 3 and 6 were in daycare.

However, there are still some inequalities in the workplace. Women do not hold an equal share of high-level positions, nor are they as well

Women's lives in the next generation will be considerably different from those of their mothers.

TO SMOKE OR NOT TO SMOKE?

Smoking in Denmark brings a clash within a society that is generally conscious about health issues and equally dedicated to preserving personal freedom. Denmark is lagging behind the growing movement in Europe to ban smoking in public spaces or workplaces. However, in 2005, Brøndby County led the way, banning smoking in all public buildings. There is a feeling the rest of the country will follow, but no date has been set.

The number of cigarette smokers has fallen since the 1980s but now remains constant at around 30 percent of the population. There has been a small increase in the number of young female smokers.

One area no campaign looks likely to challenge is the habit many older Danish women have of smoking small cigars, or cheroots.

---

represented in industry as they are in service areas such as education and health. Although by law women must be paid the same as men for doing the same work, in practice this is sometimes difficult to enforce.

With so many women working, Danish men usually play a major part in bringing up children. Yet it would be wrong to presume that the domestic roles have reached total equality. A recent magazine survey revealed that the average Danish man still does less around the house than his wife, even when both are working. In addition, when they do take on household chores, Danish men generally prefer less demanding tasks such as washing dishes.

One area where Danish women have exerted a particularly strong influence is politics. They acquired the right to vote in 1915, five years before women in the United States, and today women hold around one-third of the seats in parliament. Several political parties have women leaders, including the Christian Democratic Party, with Marianne Karlsmose, the Danish People's Party, led by Pia Kjærsgaard, and the Radical Liberal Party, led by the popular Marianne Jelved. There are also several women in the inner government, including Rikke Hvilshøj, the new Minister for Refugees, Immigrants, and Intergration; Ulla Pedersen Tørnæs, the Minister of Foreign Aid; Lene Espersen, the Minister of Justice; and Connie Hedegaard, the Minister of the Environment

Women are a particularly powerful force in referendums. It is widely believed that it was the vote of Danish women that played the decisive part in initially defeating the Maastricht Treaty.

MARRIAGE

Danes display a more relaxed attitude toward marriage than people from other European nations. It is not at all unusual for young people to live together or even start a family without being married. As many as 200,000 people have chosen to live in "paperless marriages." These are couples who have accepted all the responsibilities of being together and who are recognized as being a couple by their friends but have not gone through any religious or civil ceremony.

It is hoped that by living together first young people will see if their relationship looks likely to last before committing themselves to marriage. That is the theory, but there seems to be little evidence of it actually working, because divorce is very high in Denmark. About 30,000 Danish couples get married each year, and around 15,000 get divorced. Although marriage is no longer considered socially necessary, most couples do

A Danish couple with their child.

eventually elect to make a formal commitment to each other. However, Danes now tend to be older when they marry. Typically a man is around 36 years of age and a woman 33.

Civil weddings usually take place at the town hall and are performed by the mayor or his deputy. Church weddings are generally more traditional and elaborate. Typically the bride wears a long white dress, and the groom arrives at the church in a tuxedo or at least a formal suit. The groom selects one close friend as his best man. The bride is escorted into the church by her father or a close male relative, but it would be unusual for her to have bridesmaids. The exception might be if there are close female relatives who are still very young. As the couple leaves the church, friends throw confetti, and it is not unusual for the guests to wave tiny Danish flags.

In Denmark, homosexuals are entitled to register their partnership, which is as legally binding as a traditional marriage.

73

Property prices
in Copenhagen
are lower than
in many other
European cities,
such as London or
Paris. A medium-
sized apartment
that would cost
around $900,000
in London costs
approximately
$360,000 in
Copenhagen.

THE IMPORTANCE OF THE HOME

Unlike neighboring nations, such as Britain and Germany, where pubs, clubs, and beer cellars have traditionally been important social centers, Danish social life has always centered on the home.

Certainly most Danes are extremely "house proud" and take great care and pride in their homes. Houses are large by European standards, and in the typical family 30 percent of the income goes directly to furnishing and running the house. This includes heavy heating bills during winter.

There has been a major building program since the war, and many Danes live in houses that are less than 50 years old. The government has subsidized construction of new houses and offers maintenance grants to improve older properties. Low-income families may also qualify for a rent subsidy. The result is that slum or substandard housing hardly exists in Denmark. Instead, the pattern repeated in every Danish town is of neat rows of individual houses, with clean streets and well-kept gardens.

HOUSING

Housing is not cheap in Denmark, and rural and urban property prices can differ widely. Many couples start married life in an apartment, perhaps rented from the government. Despite close family ties, it is unusual for young Danish couples to move into the home of another family member. Many people who work in Copenhagen or other cities choose to live in surrounding villages and commute to work.

	Two-bedroom apartment	Three-bedroom house
Rural location	$75,000	$175,000
Copenhagen	$130,000	$350,000

SENIOR CITIZENS

Danish people receive a pension at 65 years of age and there are now plans to help them retire earlier. After 60, most Danes can elect to take redundancy, which means they can stop working but still receive a percentage of their salary until they qualify for their pension.

As people get older, help is provided to allow them to stay in their own homes for as long as possible. When people get too old to manage alone, they are usually given a place in a nursing home.

Most Danish senior citizens continue to lead active lives.

RELIGION

THERE ARE NO RECENT SURVEYS of religious beliefs, but it is believed that 85 percent of Danes belong to the state-supported National Church of Denmark, which is Evangelical Lutheran.

The Danish parliament has control over the National Church, but it does not interfere with religious practices. Unlike churches in many other European countries, the National Church of Denmark has no supreme spiritual leader. Church affairs are managed by 10 bishops.

Few Danes attend church regularly, and except at Christmas and Easter, there is seldom a full congregation. Similarly, it is quite unusual to hear Danes talk about religion, which is considered an area of private concern of little interest to other people. Rural and fishing communities, particularly in Jutland, tend to support the church more than urban populations.

DANES AND THE CHURCH

Church attendance in Denmark is very low. Probably only 3 to 4 percent of the members of the National Church actually attend a service on any particular Sunday. However, many people are active in other areas, such as church choirs, bible study groups, or youth clubs. Churches also get much larger attendances at Easter and Christmas.

Events such as christenings and weddings are still occasions when many Danes turn to the church. Probably 80 percent of babies are christened in church, and this number has been stable for many years. Half the weddings in Denmark still take place in church, and the church helps with most funerals.

THE HISTORY OF CHRISTIANITY IN DENMARK

The credit for converting the Danes to Christianity goes to the French monk Ansgar, known as the Apostle of the North. With the support of King Harald Bluetooth, the Roman Catholic faith was able to establish a strong following in Denmark. In the 10th and 11th centuries more than 2,000 rural churches were built in the country. The king may have been influenced by political advantage when he adopted the new religion. One of the great fears at the time was that the powerful Christian kingdoms to the south would try to invade Denmark.

Over the next 300 years, the Roman Catholic Church grew into a rich and politically powerful force. It owned many estates and farms and received a percentage of all the grain grown in the country. At the same time, the Church upset many ordinary people by allowing members of the Danish nobility to become religious officials, often solely to increase their own wealth, and support grew for Protestantism. King Frederik I, although staying loyal to the Catholic Church, invited Lutheran preachers to visit Denmark. As a result, it was this branch of Protestantism that emerged as the most popular.

The ongoing feud between Protestants and Catholics turned into civil war when King Frederik died in 1533. His elder son, Christian, favored Protestantism, whereas the younger brother, Hans, was a Catholic. After three years of fighting, the Protestants prevailed. Once in power, King Christian III quickly appointed new bishops and converted Denmark to the Lutheran religion.

Opposite: **Bishop Absalon was a powerful figure who established schools, churches, and monasteries throughout the country.**

THE VIKING GODS

The Vikings had their own religious beliefs that are still familiar today, although they are now regarded as myths and legends. The Vikings believed the gods lived in a land called Asgard. In Asgard was the Great Hall of Valhalla, where dead warriors fought all day and feasted all night in anticipation of the last great battle at the end of time. People inhabited the middle world, which was surrounded by a great uncrossable ocean. On the third level lay Nifheim, the icy world of the dead.

Odin was considered the king of the gods. He was the god of battle, but he was also a poet and able to foresee the future. His son, Thor, is the best known of the Viking gods. With his magical hammer, Mjollnir, he kept the troublesome giants at bay and wrestled with the great sea serpent that surrounded the middle world. Thor was visualized as a redbearded man of immense size, always dependable and trustworthy, although he could lose his temper quickly and was often slow to grasp the important points of an issue.

Other gods included Freyr, god of plenty, Njord, god of the seas, and the heroic Tyr.

All our knowledge of the Viking gods comes from a small collection of documents, written in the 13th century. Therefore our knowledge is neither complete nor undisputed. For example, historians question the relationship of Odin and Thor. Odin has always been considered the king of the Viking gods, yet it is Thor who gets more mention on runic stones. It is possible that the Vikings actually considered Thor to be the more important god and that later writers overemphasized the importance of Odin.

Vikings often wore a small replica of Thor's hammer, such as the one shown here, for protection from danger. Later, the molds used to make these were converted to make crosses for the new Christians.

KIERKEGAARD AND GRUNDTVIG

Two religious thinkers of the 19th century have had a profound influence on the way Danes think about religion: N. F. S. Grundtvig and Søren Kierkegaard.

N. F. S. Grundtvig (1783–1872) was responsible for a religious revival that became the major influence on the Danish Church from 1848 on. He believed that Christianity is not based on right beliefs, religious experiences, or morality, but rather on the sacraments. The word of God is to be found in the rites of baptism and communion, and in the Lord's Prayer. Grundtvig expressed his view of Christianity in his hymns, for which he is still admired.

Søren Kierkegaard (1813–55) *(depicted here on the left)* emphasized the choice everyone must make between God and the world. He argued there are no logical reasons for choosing one or the other; instead people must decide for themselves whether to make the "leap of faith" to believe in God. Anyone who asks for rational explanations or proof is trying to get around the need to make a personal decision. Kierkegaard is known today as the father of existentialism.

EVERYDAY INVOLVEMENT

Unless Danes make an objection in writing, a small percentage of their taxes are automatically paid to the church. Few Danes opt out of this contribution, as most people wish to have church support at times of marriage, birth, or death. About half the people getting married in Denmark choose to do so in church, and around 80 percent of Danish people have their children baptized.

A large number of Danes have their children confirmed. Confirmation usually takes place as children reach the seventh grade, when they are about 13 years old, and they are expected to attend six months of special classes. A successful confirmation is usually rewarded with gifts and is seen as an important step toward adulthood.

CHURCH ARCHITECTURE

Many of the churches in Denmark are 800 to 900 years old. These simple buildings give the Danish countryside much of its character. They were generally built on hilltops out of whitewashed stone, and many have medieval frescoes on the walls and ceiling. The favorite theme is a warning about the punishments facing those who live corrupt lives.

The most important cathedral in Denmark is the one at Roskilde. Bishop Absalon started the cathedral in 1170, but it was 300 years before it was finished. Extensions have been added right up to the present day. It is a large brick building and from the outside has little of the charm of the great cathedrals of France or Germany. Yet, inside the cathedral, one finds a museum of Danish history. Over 30 Danish monarchs are buried within the church, and the priceless artwork includes a statue by Bertel Thorvaldsen, one of the leading sculptors of the 19th century. A famous feature of the church is the 16th-century clock that on the hour sends out a figure of Saint George to slay the dragon.

The Grundtvig Church was designed as a tribute to N.F.S. Gruntvig, who was the most important influence on the contemporary Danish church.

Modern Danish church architecture is best represented by the Grundtvig Church in Copenhagen. Building started in 1921 and was not finished until 1940. Although it is a giant cathedral-sized structure, its unique design is inspired by Danish country churches. The façade recalls the shape of an organ, a tribute to the hundreds of hymns Grundtvig composed.

THE CHURCH COMMUNITY

Churches in Denmark are often very active within their communities. In addition to their religious duties, vicars carry out considerable social work. A great deal of effort goes into attracting children to the church; in addition to confirmation classes, many churches run their own youth clubs. Women are fully accepted and make up over 10 percent of the nation's clergy. On Sunday, services are broadcast over the radio for those unable to come to church. Many Danes prefer to listen to these broadcasts in their own home rather than attending a public church service.

Whitewashed churches dot the Danish countryside.

MANY RELIGIONS

Muslims make up the second largest religious group in Denmark. However, the customs of some Muslim groups, such as arranged marriages, can cause conflict in Danish society. There are also fears that small radical elements might make the nation more vulnerable to terrorism or inspire attacks on its small Jewish population. Although Muslims are growing in number, there are few mosques in Denmark, and these tend to be in converted buildings. There were hopes of building a large mosque in northwestern Copenhagen but the plan was never fulfilled.

Around 35,000 Roman Catholics make up the third largest religious group in Denmark. Other Christian groups include the Swedish Church, the Russian Orthodox Church, and the Reform Church.

There is a small, long-established Jewish community. Jews have little trouble integrating into their local community. There might be family conflicts when a Jew marries a Christian, although even here Danish tolerance and belief in individual freedom are likely to prevail.

LANGUAGE

DANISH IS SPOKEN by about 6 million people in Denmark, the Faeroe Islands, and Greenland. When Danish is written, it is a single, formal language, although in spoken form it has several dialects.

Danish is closely related to Swedish and Norwegian. In fact, Danes and Norwegians can usually understand each other if they speak slowly and clearly. When written, these two languages are even more similar, since they share a large vocabulary but differ in pronunciation. Swedish, has significant differences. Both Swedish and Norwegian are taught in schools starting in the seventh grade. English is taught even earlier.

The predominant language on Greenland is Greenlandic, which is closely related to languages spoken by the Inuit of northern Canada, Alaska, and Siberia. Because few of the resident Danes learn Greenlandic, Danish is widely used in teaching, administration, and business. Many young people also understand English.

The Faeroe Islanders speak Faeroese, a Scandinavian language closely related to Icelandic and Norwegian. In the 16th century, Faeroese fell into disuse as a written language but survived as a vehicle for a rich oral literature, including sagas and poems sung to folk dances. In the mid-19th century, a written Faeroese language was created, but it was not until 1937 that it was used in the schools and 1948 in legal institutions. There is a body of literature in Faeroese, and eight newspapers are published in the language.

THE HISTORY OF DANISH

About 4,000 years ago, the early settlers of Scandinavia still spoke the same language as the tribes living farther south in Germany. Over many hundreds of years the language spoken in Scandinavia slowly changed until it became quite different from the Germanic language it had started out as. All the basic words still came from the old German language, but there were now so many words borrowed from Greek and Latin that a new, Scandinavian language had emerged.

By the 12th century Danish started to diverge from the language spoken in Sweden. At this time Denmark ruled Norway and so had considerable influence over the people there. This is one reason why the Danish and Norwegian languages are still so similar today.

The earliest manuscripts appeared during the 14th century. Most of these recorded local laws but are particularly important to students of language because they show that there were various written dialects used in different parts of Denmark.

The Jelling Stone contains an inscription on one side and a design on the other.

THE INFLUENCE OF DANISH

The Viking expansion resulted in a number of Scandinavian-speaking settlements that left their mark on their neighbors. Iceland and the Faeroe Islands continue to speak a dialect of Scandinavian today. Colonies in the Hebrides, the Isle of Man, Ireland, the Danelaw in England, and Normandy in France stopped speaking Scandinavian after a short time, while the Orkneys and Scottish coasts continued until about 1700 and the Shetlands until 1750.

The Danish colonization of the Danelaw has resulted in many Scandinavian words being incorporated into English. For example, "law," "by-law," "fellow," "skull," "skin," "sky," "window," "birth," and "thrift" all come from Scandinavian.

The first evidence of writing in Denmark dates from A.D. 200. These first inscriptions used the ancient runic alphabet and were carved onto stones or wooden boards. At first there were 24 runic letters, but by 900 only 16 letters were still in common use.

When printed books started to appear at the end of the 15th century, it became important to have a common version of the written language. It was the dialect used in Copenhagen, the seat of government, which became recognized as standard Danish. Another important influence was the first translation of the Bible, because the grammar and spelling used in the translation became the standard.

It was not until the 18th century that modern rules of grammar started to be accepted in the way they are used today. Spelling took even longer to develop into the standard modern form, but in 1889 the government finally adopted spelling rules to be used nationwide.

In modern times Danish has borrowed words from other sources, particularly from French, German, and English. Most musical and banking terms derive from Italian, the bulk of the cooking and women's fashion terms from French, a large number of maritime words from Dutch, and scientific terminology chiefly from the classical languages. Words are borrowed to describe technical or scientific terms that do not exist in Danish. We see this clearly demonstrated in computer language. Danes use the term "hard disk" because there is no direct translation. However, when computer manuals talk about memory they use *hukommelse*, the Danish word for memory.

Standard Danish is spoken mainly by television news reporters.

DIALECTS

Although written Danish was largely standardized by the start of this century, numerous versions of the spoken language still existed, particularly in rural communities. Today there are three main dialects, those of western Jutland, the central islands, and Bornholm. The Jutland dialect differs the most from the rest of the Danish dialects. People from Jutland who have a heavy accent might even have some problem making themselves understood in Copenhagen. Under the influence of radio and television, the dialects are dying out, replaced by a standard Danish. This educated Danish is called *rigsdansk* (RIJ-dansk); in its pure form, it is only spoken by television reporters and a few people from the middle classes. The vast majority of Danes speak a version of *rigsdansk* influenced by their regional accent.

THE ALPHABET

Danish has three extra letters compared to the Roman alphabet. An ordinary *a* is pronounced as the *a* in the word "bar," but *å* sounds like the *a* in "paw." The letter *æ* makes the same sound as the *e* in "egg." The special *ø* is pronounced like the *u* in "turn."

In addition some of the other letters of the alphabet are not pronounced the same way they would be in English. The letter *j* is pronounced as the English *y*, and *w* as *v*.

The letters *ø* and *å (right, a signboard showing the letter ø)* have only been written in this form for the

last 40 years. Before this, the *ø* was written as *oe* and the *å* as *aa*. Some Danish people still insist on using the old version, particularly with place names. *Ålborg*, for example, can often be found written as *Aalborg*.

COUNTING IN DANISH

0	*nul* (nool)		6	*seks* (sehks)
1	*en* (en)		7	*syv* (SEE-oo)
2	*to* (toh)		8	*otte* (AW-der)
3	*tre* (tray)		9	*ni* (nee)
4	*fire* (FEE-rer)		10	*ti* (tee)
5	*fem* (fehm)			

Danes name larger numbers in a way similar to French, which becomes quite complex if one stops to think about their meaning. Seventy, for example, is *halvfjerds* (HALF-ee-as), which literally means three times 20 plus half of 20.

Copenhagen's National Library houses an excellent collection of books in various languages.

THE IMPORTANCE OF A SECOND LANGUAGE

English-speaking travelers in Denmark get so used to Danish people being able to understand them that they are often surprised when they finally meet a Dane who does not speak English well.

Learning another language is very important to Danes. Business people need to speak English when dealing with overseas customers, and students in higher education need to refer to studies and books written in English. It is estimated that 57 percent of the general population and 97 percent of university graduates speak English. In public libraries, Danish and English books are mixed together on the shelves.

Because Germany is both a close neighbor and an important trading partner, many Danes also learn German. In the areas where Jutland borders Germany, most Danes are able to communicate in German.

DANISH NAMES

Some 850,000 Danes share the three most common surnames of Jensen, Nielsen, and Hansen. In fact, two-thirds of all Danish people have a surname that ends in *-sen* (meaning son), including the Pedersens, Larsens, Andersens, Christensens, and Petersens.

Fashions in given names have changed over the last few years. Traditional Danish given names frequently borrow saints' names. Names such as Kirsten, Maria, or Marianne for girls and Peter, Hans, or Søren for boys have now lost much of their old popularity. Emma, Julie, and Mathilde are now extremely popular names for girls, with Mikkel, Frederik, Mathias, Mads, and Rasmus becoming increasingly common for boys.

There is also a trend for people to give their children more original names, such as Pi or Pil. Rebecca, seldom used in Denmark until 10 years ago, has become popular. It is also common, particularly with girls, to join two names together, as in Anne-Mette or Anne-Louise.

Two names that look likely to survive any changing fashion are the royal names of Christian and Frederik, which remain as popular as ever.

The Danes tend to be informal. The formal mode of address *De* has more or less been abolished. Inherited and social titles are not taken very seriously, but earned titles such as doctor and titles indicating a person's position in business or government are generally used.

Probably the most used word in the Danish language is *tak* ("tahk"). It can mean "thank you," "please," or "excuse me," and sometimes seems to be added to every sentence you hear!

ARTS

THE EARLIEST KNOWN human images found in Denmark were carved on a 10,000-year-old aurochs bone, but it was during the Viking period that a distinctive culture emerged. The Viking period achieved great developments in the arts. Carpenters, blacksmiths, and other craftspeople excelled, producing finely decorated weapons, drinking horns, musical instruments, and jewelry.

The first Danish musical instrument was the *lur* (luhr), a long, curving, horn-shaped instrument that produced a hoarse, sonorous, trumpet-like sound. Many of these beautiful instruments have been found in Viking graves.

The skilled decoration on weapons, tools, and ornaments indicates ancient traditions of art and metalworking. Viking design is characterized by ornamentation consisting of ingeniously intertwined animals.

The Viking period also produced the first written records of Danish history, which were carved in runes onto large stones or wooden boards. The true runic period was 900–1050, but there are inscriptions of various kinds from several hundred years before and 200 years after.

The Viking period is described in the *Gesta Danorum* by Saxo Grammaticus. Written in Latin around 1200, its 16 books range from legendary history to chronicles of the author's own time. A defender of royalty, Saxo promotes the virtues of loyalty, moderation, and courage.

Above: **A craftsperson working on the famous Royal Copenhagen pottery.**

Opposite: **A show during celebrations for the 200th anniversary of Hans Christian Andersen.**

Karen Blixen, who wrote under the name of Isak Dinesen, was known for her *Seven Gothic Tales* and *Out of Africa*. During her years in Kenya, Blixen learned Swahili and grew to love the country and its people. Here she is holding her servant's son a year before the failure of her coffee plantation forced her to return to Denmark.

WRITERS

Ludvig Holberg (1684–1754) was a scholar known for his many comedies as well as histories and essays. His liberal humanism has been of lasting importance to Danish culture. His works advocate relativism and tolerance, practical common sense coupled with social responsibility.

Hans Christian Andersen and Søren Kierkegaard dominated the 19th century. Martin Andersen Nexø won international fame with *Pelle the Conqueror*, which portrayed the humble people of his native Bornholm. Johannes Jensen was inspired by the doctrine of evolution in his short prose, novels, and lyrics. He won the Nobel Prize in literature in 1944.

Peter Hoeg is the best known contemporary Danish writer. In the 1990s he had international success with *Miss Smilla's Sense of Snow*, which examined the treatment of Greenlanders and portrayed Danish social services as harsh. The only other modern writer to equal his achievements is Ib Michael, who used his experience of traveling in Central America to create stories such as *The Prince* (1997) and *The Emperor's Atlas* (2001), which combine imagination and reality almost like a modern fairy tale.

HANS CHRISTIAN ANDERSEN

Hans Christian Andersen is unarguably Denmark's most famous son. Andersen was born to a poor family in Odense in 1805. His father was a shoemaker, and his mother wanted Hans to find a similar trade, perhaps as a tailor. Andersen, however, was convinced he was destined to become famous and, at the age of 14, set out to Copenhagen to seek his fortune as an actor and singer. The young man did have a fine voice, but after several years in the capital he had still not found employment in the theater. Instead Andersen started to write, and when he was 24 he published a collection of stories and then a play. Neither was a great success, and Andersen left Denmark to travel around Europe. While in Italy he wrote a novel called *The Improvisatore*. Although set in Rome, this was in fact the story of Andersen's own childhood. The book became popular in Denmark and was soon published in England and Germany.

Andersen had already been working on a collection of four fairy stories, and these were published a few weeks after his novel. The book was badly printed on poor paper and was not well received by the critics. Fortunately, a few close friends encouraged Andersen to continue writing his fairy stories, and from then on he brought out a new volume every Christmas. Included in these little booklets were *The Little Mermaid*, *The Ugly Duckling*, and *The Emperor's New Clothes*, stories that made Andersen famous around the world. His fairy tales have been translated into more than 100 languages.

Andersen never married and lived in furnished rooms or hotels all his life. He was an avid traveler, making 29 journeys in Europe. His childhood home in Odense is now a museum.

Andersen's fairy tales, based on a belief in living miracles, combine a complex sense of humor that exposes pettiness and egotism with a firm belief in eternal justice. His writing shows extraordinary sensitivity and subtlety, but these qualities tend, unfortunately, to be lost in translations.

Jazz players entertain on a canal boat in Copenhagen.

MUSIC

Danes enjoy all types of music from classical to pop. Denmark has two operas and seven fully developed symphony orchestras. Danmarks Radio, the national broadcasting corporation, runs several orchestras and choirs. There are five regional orchestras, and many of these play new classical music composed by Danes. The best known of all Denmark's classical musicians is Carl Nielsen.

Most cities and even some small towns will have at least one hall that provides live music. Jazz music is extremely popular and the best Danish musicians, such as trumpeter Palle Mikkelborg or the late bass player Niels-Henning Ørsted Pedersen, are famous throughout the world. There are summer music festivals, the most important being the Roskilde rock festival and the Copenhagen jazz festival. Opera has become increasingly popular; seldom is there an empty seat in the Royal Theatre in Copenhagen or the Danish National Opera in Århus. In 2005 Copenhagen opened a waterfront opera house.

CARL NIELSEN Carl Nielsen was born in a village south of Odense in 1865, near the birthplace of Hans Christian Andersen. Like Andersen, he was from a poor family and left for Copenhagen to seek his fortune. And like Andersen, he was successful. During his long career, Nielsen wrote six symphonies, two operas, a variety of concertos, piano compositions, and quartets, many choral works, an organ work, and many ballads.

At his 60th birthday banquet, Nielsen told the audience that his mother had always said to him, "Don't forget that Hans Christian Andersen was poor like you." With that inspiration, Nielsen became a composer of international stature. From his father, he learned the music of Hayden and Mozart and the traditional airs of his native Fyn Island; he incorporated both in his compositions. After studying at the Copenhagen Conservatory, he joined the Royal Orchestra as a violinist and eventually became its conductor. He later taught at the Conservatory and became its director shortly before his death.

DANISH POP MUSIC

Danish pop is heavily influenced by fashions and trends in the United States and Britain. Danish pop stars perform in Danish or English and are quite likely to switch languages with each song.

The most famous of Denmark's pop artists is Kim Larsen, now a veteran of many years in the business, but still as outrageous as ever. Popular Danish acts have included Aqua and the classically-trained Safri Duo. Recent rock sensations are Kashmir, Saybia, and Carpark North.

PAINTING AND SCULPTURE

Danish painting has a distinctiveness that sets it apart from European painting in general. It is characterized by a quiet intimacy, combined with a deep love of and respect for nature, and an always apparent, instinctive dislike of extremes and heroics. A distaste for sentimentality and vulgar emotional display is evident in the tone of restrained simplicity.

Modern art in Denmark traces its roots to the early part of the 19th century. The most important figure of this period is C.W. Eckersberg, who is considered the father of Danish painting. Like most artists of his day Eckersberg made a grand tour, living and painting in Paris and Rome, where he learned a strictly objective, penetrating, almost microscopic

A modern sculpture at an intersection in Fyn. Danish sculptors continue to produce some of the country's most exciting and original pieces, with Robert Jacobsen leading the way with his unique iron sculptures.

BERTEL THORVALDSEN

Bertel Thorvaldsen is the only Danish visual artist to have achieved worldwide fame. The son of an Icelandic woodcarver who had settled in Denmark, he was born in Copenhagen and studied at the Copenhagen Academy, where he won a scholarship to Rome. He found success with his statue *Jason* when he was still a student in Rome, and stayed there for 40 years. His restrained classicism earned him an international reputation as the foremost sculptor of his time and he had one of the most spectacularly successful careers of the 19th century. His return to Copenhagen in 1838 was regarded as a national event in Danish history.

Thorvaldsen excluded dramatic expression from his work in order to achieve an ideal beauty. Although his works were once regarded as the perfect reincarnation of classical art, they now seem somewhat cold.

The little town of Skagen on the very tip of northern Jutland has always held a special place with Danish artists who are attracted there by the solitude, the beauty of the area, and the special light. Skagen artists are naturally inspired to produce scenes of sea and sky, and some of their best work can be seen in the local museum.

study of nature. Eckersberg then returned to Denmark, where he spent 35 years teaching at the Royal Academy of Art in Copenhagen.

The generation of artists trained by Eckersberg created the golden period of Danish painting. Christen Købke is one of the best-known painters of this age; when one of his paintings recently came on the market, the National Gallery in London purchased it for over $390,000.

The 19th century is dominated by the sculptor Bertel Thorvaldsen, who achieved international fame during his lifetime. Today there is a museum in Copenhagen dedicated to Thorvaldsen's work.

Erik Frandsen is one of the most respected artists of the present generation. His work ranges from a swirling mass of colors to paintings such as *Portrait of Ester*, in which automobile tires are incorporated into the picture to give it depth and texture. Lars Norgard, with thought-provoking works such as *Mod lyset*, and Claus Carstensen, who often works with foam, are among today's other top artists.

The Louisiana Museum in northern Zealand has one of the leading collections of modern art in Europe. During the 1990s several Danish artists became noted for their video art. Video art often focuses on a personal story, but some artists prefer to do documentary work. Women artists have been very successful in making Danish videos.

Postal stamps proudly display Danish design.

DESIGN

Danish designers are renowned for making household objects interesting and attractive as well as functional. This appreciation of good design is very much a part of Danish culture, and it has been said that every Danish home is a miniature modern art museum. Danish furniture, lamps, silverware, pottery, toys, and fabrics often win international design awards.

Foremost among designers is Hans Wegner, who with his famous furniture has been described as the founder of modern Danish design. Other key figures include Kay Bojesen, who is best known for his tableware; pottery master Christian Poulsen; and Poul Henningsen, whose modern lamps set the standard for a whole generation of young designers.

Danish porcelain is particularly famous, with the Royal Copenhagen, the Holmegaard Glass Factory, and the Bing and Grondahl factory producing some of the world's finest serving porcelain and decorative china.

The Royal Copenhagen reputation was originally built around one dinner service. In the 1780s King Frederik ordered a 1,800-piece service as a gift for Catherine II of Russia. Each piece was handmade and decorated with paintings of Danish plants and flowers, and the set took 15 years to make. The empress died before the gift was completed, and so the set was never sent to Russia. This one project established the international reputation of both the Royal Copenhagen and the Danish porcelain industry. Since then, Denmark has earned acclaim for producing fine porcelain.

ARCHITECTURE

The gift for design is reflected in the work of Danish architects. Professor Arne Jacobsen is considered the first of the great modern architects. Several of his buildings, including the SAS Hotel and the Danish Central Bank, are important Copenhagen landmarks.

Many top Danish architects have produced their finest work overseas: the parliament building in Kuwait; the foreign ministry building in Saudi Arabia; the new Saint Catherine's College (by Arne Jacobsen) in Oxford; and the Grande Arche (by Johann Otto von Spreckelsen) in Paris.

The Planetarium in Copenhagen, with its unique cylindrical shape, is one of the finest examples of modern Danish architecture. The new Copenhagen Opera House, at the entrance to the port, was designed by Henning Larsens Tegnestue, who had already designed several famous buildings in the city.

Jørgen Utzon designed the Sydney Opera House in Sydney, Australia, considered a masterpiece of modern architecture.

The Copenhagen Royal Theater is home to the state ballet, theater, and opera companies.

DANCE AND THEATER

The Copenhagen Royal Theater in the center of Copenhagen is home to the state ballet, theater, and opera companies. Of these, the Royal Danish Ballet Company has the strongest international reputation. During the 1830s the great French director August Bournonville settled in Denmark, and under his inspiration the company established a magnificent repertoire of dances. The Royal Danish Ballet Company still performs many of these classical dances today but complements them with an exciting program of original modern ballets. This versatility is one reason the company is so admired. They have been invited to dance in theaters around the world, including performances in the United States, Japan, and China.

In 1988 the Royal Ballet held a dance festival at which the first Hans Christian Andersen Ballet Awards were presented. It is hoped that these awards will become the ballet version of the Oscars.

Copenhagen supports between eight and 10 theaters, and there are also permanent theaters in most provincial cities. Smaller towns are visited by traveling troupes, and one Danish drama group turned an old barge into a floating theater!

Theater offers limited opportunities for modern Danish writers, many of whom also write for television. The government sponsors Danish theater by subsidizing organizations that make tickets available to the public at reduced prices. A unique part of the amateur drama scene consists of Viking plays. These often involve 200 to 300 local people who work with a professional director to reenact scenes from Viking legends.

FILM

At the turn of the century, during the age of the silent movie, the Danish film industry became notorious for tackling daring subjects, often with a sexual theme. In addition to being provocative, Danish movies could also be beautiful. Carl Th. Dreyer's *La Passion de Jeanne d'Arc* is considered one of the best silent movies ever made.

Danish filmmakers produce around 16 major movies each year, including such Oscar-winning films as *Babette's Feast* (1988) and *Pelle the Conqueror* (1989). The latter made director Bille August famous. In 1995 Lars von Trier and Thomas Vinterberg started the Dogme movement, which uses only handheld camera and no props or special effects. The main idea was to avoid established film genres. Lars von Trier has become Denmark's most talked about director. His best-known film is *Dogville*, which starred Nicole Kidman.

A multi-screen cinema in Copenhagen shows Hollywood movies as well as Danish productions.

LEISURE

MOST PEOPLE IN DENMARK work a five-day week, leaving the weekends free. In addition, the long summer days allow ample time to participate in outdoor activities during the evenings. Danish people generally make use of this free time to enjoy a variety of hobbies and sports.

A nation that spends so much of the winter in the cold and dark is particularly anxious to get outdoors as soon as the warmer weather arrives. Therefore sailing and cycling have always been popular. Recently, more and more Danes have followed the international trend and become avid joggers. There are local races every weekend, and the Copenhagen marathon now attracts 4,000 runners.

The Danish countryside, with its numerous walking and riding trails, is another source of relaxation. Trails are well maintained and marked, and there are many local walking societies that offer organized hikes. The winter season brings its own activities. The Danes are avid skaters. On weekends many people simply enjoy walking through the frosty countryside. Chess and bridge are popular games.

Most people enjoy five weeks of vacation a year, and each summer thousands of Danes fly south to the beaches of Italy and Spain. Denmark was one of the first countries to pioneer the idea of "package vacations." It is also quite common for Danish people to take several months off work, usually just after finishing their studies, to travel to more distant parts of the world, with Thailand and India being popular destinations.

Above: **The Roskilde Music Festival draws thousands of spectators.**

Opposite: **Marathon runners cross the Øresund Bridge.**

Danish fans jokingly call themselves *roligans* (ROHL-ee-gans), which combines the Danish word *rolig*, which means "quiet," with the English word "hooligans."

A COMMITMENT TO SPORTS

The oldest athletic club in Denmark was founded in 1892. Four years later Denmark was one of a handful of nations represented at the first modern Olympic Games. The country won eight medals at the last Olympics in sports such as rowing, sailing, table tennis, badminton, team handball, and track and field.

Although soccer is the most popular sport, badminton has brought Denmark the most international success. Flemming Delfs and Lene Koppen were winners of the men's and women's titles at the first world championship in 1977. The rise of Asian players has prevented Denmark from winning further world titles, but they still rank as one of the strongest nations in Europe. Other world champions include badminton players Peter Gade and Camilla Martin.

Speedway (motorbike races around a narrow cinder track) is another sport where Denmark has excelled. Hans Nielsen, with 19 world titles, is the most successful speedway racer of all time.

SOCCER

Denmark was one of the first countries in the world to take the British game of soccer seriously, and by the turn of the century the Danish team was considered the best on mainland Europe. However, once the larger European nations started to organize professional leagues, Denmark could no longer compete. It was not until the late 1980s that Denmark again built up a strong national team. The main reason for their recent success is that all the best Danish players play for professional clubs in Germany, Italy, or Britain.

Danish soccer teams have become used to qualifying for major tournaments and doing well. However, the only time Denmark won a tournament was in 1992 when they became European champions. Ironically the team had not qualified for the finals that year, but had been invited to take part at late notice when Yugoslavia withdrew. The Danish players rushed back from their holiday and went on to beat Germany 2–0 in the final.

Soccer quickly became the national game, and it remains the most popular sport today, with around 300,000 registered players of all ages.

BICYCLING

Bicycling is a favorite family activity on summer weekends. Because Denmark is a flat country with beautiful scenery, it is ideal for cycling. And when the weather is nice, a bicycle tour is a pleasant way to get out and enjoy the scenery.

As well as being a pleasant form of recreation, bicycling is also a major means of transportation in Denmark. Many families have bicycles, and cycling is considered both good exercise and environmentally friendly. Even in Copenhagen, bicycles can be seen everywhere, and they are often the best means of transportation.

Denmark's country lanes are quiet and peaceful, and most major roads have bicycle lanes. Within towns and cities there are elaborate systems of bicycle paths, often with their own stoplights and road signs. Automobiles are required to give way to bicycles.

There are specially marked cars on the trains for storing bicycles, and bicycle parking lots are found everywhere. Another interesting Danish idea is the coin-operated air pump found outside many stores. In Copenhagen 37 percent of the city's inhabitants cycle to work.

WATER SPORTS

The Danes traditionally have a special love for the sea, and sailing draws enormous numbers of enthusiasts. Yachting has the strongest following in northern Zealand, where many of the best natural harbors are situated.

Denmark's enthusiasm for sailing, rowing, and cycling has helped win a steady flow of Olympic medals. This total has now passed 150, a record better than many larger countries. Denmark has also produced several Olympic sailing champions. The most famous is Paul Elvstrom, a legend in Denmark and winner of four Olympic medals.

The classic domestic race is the Round Zealand Regatta, which attracts 2,000 boats every year. The contesting boats gather opposite Kronborg Castle for the start. The race lasts between two and three days and covers 220 nautical miles.

Other water sports make use of Denmark's many lakes and fjords. Rowing and canoeing are popular, and many young Danes are turning just as enthusiastically to windsurfing.

Fishing, in either fresh or salt water, has a large following, with Jutland being the favorite location.

PAUL ELVSTROM, OLYMPIC YACHTSMAN

Paul Elvstrom is probably the greatest Olympic yacht racer of all time, and he won four consecutive gold medals in the Finn class. His Olympic debut came at the 1948 games in London where he failed to finish in the first race of the series. He didn't panic, and a string of high places over the rest of the week secured his first gold medal. In 1952 and 1960 Elvstrom was so far ahead of the other competitors that he did not even need to turn out for the last race of the series.

TELEVISION

Danes spend about 40 percent of their leisure time watching television. The national broadcasting corporation, DR (Danmarks Radio), has no advertising but is financed by license fees. It broadcasts a wide range of popular programs as well as more cultural programs.

With satellite and cable there are now private channels, such as TV3, which broadcasts foreign and sports programs. In some parts of the country, it is usually possible to tune in to German or Swedish channels. Danes can also watch foreign channels on cable. Sometimes these are adapted for Danish needs. For example, *Eurosport* includes Danish commentary, while foreign programs might be given Danish subtitles.

The Danes produce some of their own television programs, and these are improving in quality. One example is *Unit One*, a Danish police series that has won international awards.

TILTING THE RING

A favorite sport in southern Jutland is tilting the ring. Tilting is a colorful event, with riders dressed in their best equestrian clothes. Events are staged in different towns throughout the summer months and draw many enthusiastic competitors and hundreds of spectators.

Riders use a long pole resembling a medieval lance to hook rings that are suspended above the ground. There are 24 rings, each slightly smaller as the riders pass down the course.

TIVOLI GARDENS

Tivoli, in the center of Copenhagen, is one of the symbols of Denmark. It covers only two or three blocks, but within this space there are restaurants, theaters, bandstands, concert halls, and a museum.

Many Copenhagen residents buy a season ticket and visit the gardens several times each week. Around 4 million visitors pass through the gates each year during the four summer months when Tivoli is open.

Tivoli had its 150th anniversary in 1993; to celebrate the event an 89-foot-long (27-m) replica of a sailing ship was placed in the central lake and served as a floating restaurant.

CHESS

The Danes have been chess players for many centuries. There are stories of Viking kings playing the game while resting between raids, and chess pieces have been found in remains from the Viking period.

The most famous international competitor is Bent Larsen, who gained the title of grand master at the age of 21. In 1967 he set a world record by winning six international tournaments in succession.

Theme parks are growing increasingly popular in Denmark. One of the most interesting is Legoland in central Jutland. Here one can wander around scale models of the most famous buildings of Denmark or view a 66-foot-high (20-m) version of Mount Rushmore, all constructed out of plastic toy bricks.

FESTIVALS

DANES ENJOY SEVERAL national holidays, mostly religious, with Christmas being the most important. There are also numerous annual festivals and cultural and sporting events, such as the big yacht races, which create great excitement locally or even nationally.

In addition, special celebrations are staged on important historical anniversaries. There are also numerous flag days when the Danish flag is flown from official buildings and private homes. Many of these mark historical events or royal birthdays.

Opposite: **A display of fireworks after the wedding of Crown Prince Frederik and Australian Mary Donaldson.**

NATIONAL HOLIDAYS IN DENMARK

January 1	New Year's Day
March/April	Palm Sunday (Sunday before Easter)
March/April	Maundy Thursday (Thursday before Easter)
March/April	Good Friday (Friday before Easter)
March/April	Easter
March/April	Easter Monday
April/May	Common Prayer Day (fourth Friday after Easter)
May	Ascension Day (40th day after Easter)
May/June	Whit Sunday (50th day after Easter)
May/June	Whit Monday
June 5	Constitution Day
December 24	Christmas Eve
December 25	Christmas Day
December 26	Second Christmas Day

Other important annual events include the Copenhagen Carnival, the Round Fyn Yacht Race, the Round Zealand Yacht Race, Midsummer's Night, the Frederikssund Viking Festival, the Copenhagen Jazz Festival, the Århus Jazz Festival, and the Hans Christian Andersen Festival.

Traditional dancing at a local festival in County Rentmeester.

SPECIAL DAYS IN DANISH CULTURE

There are several holidays that are specially related to Danish culture.

Midsummer is a tradition dating back to Viking times. Bonfires are an important part of the day, a tradition that recalls the burning of witches many centuries ago. Today a life-sized model of a witch, made by stuffing old clothes full of paper or rags, is placed on top of the fire. Midsummer is a favorite time for a family barbecue.

Fastalvn (fasta-laon) takes place in February, before the fasting leading up to Easter begins. Nowadays it is considered a holiday for children. A special *Fastalvn* event is a game called "beating a cat out of the barrel." In this game a wooden barrel full of gifts is hung from a tree, and children line up to hit it with sticks. Once it breaks, the presents cascade down and are divided up. The barrel game has a cruel history, for long ago a cat would have been placed inside, and the barrel hit until the poor creature was dead. Today the game is played with candy and fruit, usually decorated with pictures of black cats. *Fastalvn* is also a day for children to wear fancy dress costumes. These often reflect favorites from the latest movies, such as *Harry Potter* or *Batman*.

On the queen's birthday, residents of Copenhagen, particularly children and the elderly, gather outside the palace. The queen traditionally comes onto the balcony just before midday to say a few words to the crowd. In return she is greeted with nine cheers.

Constitution Day is on June 5 and celebrates the adoption of the new constitution in 1849. It is usually a half-day holiday and is a particularly important day for politicians, who are kept busy with numerous political speeches and meetings.

Another historic celebration is Liberation Eve on May 4. This commemorates the end of the German occupation in 1945. On this night Danes place a lighted candle in their windows. Liberation Eve generally means more to older people, who still remember the war years.

The Copenhagen Carnival takes place in May and was originally a religious festival, although the religious importance has been more or less forgotten. The celebrations and street parties are scattered around different neighborhoods, and many people put on fancy dress costumes.

Common Prayer Day is held on the fourth Friday after Easter. People eat hot wheat buns, and then many families go for a walk. In Copenhagen a popular walk is the Kastellet where the crowds listen to a student choir.

Lunchtime at an agricultural show in Fyn.

115

Participants at the Santa Claus World Congress in Copenhagen.

CHRISTMAS

The first signs of Christmas arriving are lights and decorations going up in the center of town. Shops add their own Christmas window displays.

The evening of December 23, sometimes called "little Christmas Eve," is the traditional time for families to decorate their homes with a Christmas tree hung with lights, stars, hearts, tiny Danish flags, and Christmas figures. Much of this would be familiar to visitors from the United States, but candles play a more important role in the Danish decorations than they do in other cultures. The Nisse (NISS-ah) also add a special Danish touch to the celebration.

For children, Christmas Eve is the most important day of the celebration because this is when they receive their presents. The early evening starts with carols around the tree. One of the adults is likely to disappear for a few moments to dress up in a red cloak and white beard because it is traditional in Denmark for children to receive their presents directly from Santa Claus.

There is a special dinner on Christmas Eve. The meal starts with a special rice pudding called *ris a l'mande* (rihs-ALAH-man-tah). One whole almond is placed in the mixture, and there is a special gift put aside for whoever finds it. The main course is goose, duck, or crispy pork. Pork was once eaten only by families who could not afford anything better, but now it has become a Christmas Eve favorite.

Christmas day is often quieter and more for the adults. Many families attend a church service in the morning, even if they do not go to church at other times of the year. Children spend the day visiting friends and playing with their new Christmas gifts. Christmas dinner, served early in the afternoon, is likely to be a buffet with all the family's favorite foods.

NEW YEAR'S

At around 6:00 P.M. on the last day of the year, the queen appears on television to give her New Year speech. This is an important event for Danes, and most try to watch the yearly telecast.

On New Year's Eve children are allowed, even expected, to engage in a few naughty but harmless tricks. An old favorite was to push firecrackers through mailboxes, although this is now discouraged as being too dangerous. The family flagpole remains a likely target for New Year tricks, and many parents wake up in the morning to find a chair or the old Christmas tree suspended from the top of the pole.

THE NISSE

The Nisse are dwarflike creatures who have been part of Danish folklore since pagan times. Traditionally the Nisse are portrayed as little old men with gray beards. They were originally farm dwellers who lived in barns and outhouses. Although everybody knew the Nisse were there, they were never seen, expect perhaps for a fleeting glimpse out of the corner of the eye. As long as nobody upset them, the Nisse usually did no harm but lived side by side with their human neighbors.

In the last 100 years, these half-feared spirits of the farmyard have become increasingly associated with Christmas. The once shy Nisse now seem happy to appear in store displays, on Christmas cards, or as decorations in homes. The Nisse have changed their image as a result of their new role and are now shown as young, clean-shaven, elf-like figures.

Nisse have become so much a part of the Christmas holiday that few people associate them with any other time of the year.

Demonstrating the traditional art of lacemaking at the Kniple Festival in Tønder.

EASTER

The religious importance of Easter has faded, but the holiday is still important in Denmark as a celebration marking the end of the long, dark winter and the start of spring.

The actual holidays are Maundy Thursday, Good Friday, Easter Sunday, and Easter Monday. This long holiday makes it possible for families to visit relatives or friends who live in other parts of Denmark. Adults exchange gifts of flowers, particularly tulips and daffodils. Daffodils are in fact sometimes referred to as Easter lilies. Children receive gifts of chocolate Easter eggs, the hollow insides filled with a collection of sweets.

Young Danish children are told the story of the Easter rabbit who comes into the garden to hide eggs for them. Many Danish parents hide chocolate eggs all over the garden, and seeing the children hunt for them is part of the holiday fun. If the weather interferes, the game can be moved indoors.

Families wishing to follow a traditional celebration make eggs an important part of the holiday meals. Hardboiled eggs start the day for breakfast, and children spend hours coloring and decorating the shells. "Soiled eggs," which are hardboiled eggs in mustard sauce, are eaten later in the day. Lamb is usually the main Easter meal.

An agricultural show cow parade draws some lovely contestants in Fyn.

CARNIVALS

The summer months are busy with festivals and carnivals. Agricultural shows remain important events, as the Danes have never forgotten their farming past. Besides parades of prize farm animals, agricultural shows also attract numerous crafts stalls. Each June, Roskilde stages the biggest agricultural show in northern Europe, with over 2,000 animals on parade.

Special antique fairs also attract large crowds, as do horse fairs and crafts shows.

Most towns have their own special carnival day with a street parade, fun fair, and cultural events. For towns by the sea, the carnival often centers around the harbor. The anniversary of a city's founding or a famous person's birthday inspires special celebrations, with parades, sporting events, exhibitions, concerts, plays, and guided tours. Not only are such events a way for Danish people to enjoy themselves, but they are good for tourism and local commerce. Odense stages a famous Hans Christian Andersen festival each year that attracts visitors from all over the world.

FOOD

MOST DANES LIKE to get home early from work to enjoy a long evening with their family. Breakfast and lunch are often eaten quickly with little fuss. The evening meal, in contrast, is an important occasion for the family to spend time together.

The Danes say that "meals are for being together, not just for filling up!" The appearance of the table, the atmosphere in the room, and above all the company will be just as important in making a meal a success as the food itself.

It is polite in Denmark to begin eating as soon as the meal is ready and not to let it get cold while waiting for late guests to arrive or for a television show to end. Guests are always encouraged to take second portions.

Left: **A bread shop window displays various traditional breads.**

Opposite: **Herring is Denmark's national dish.**

TYPICAL MEALS

A traditional meal centered around meatballs and potatoes.

In addition to herring, Danes are also particularly fond of pork, soup, meatballs, and above all the sandwiches known as *smørrebrød* (SMEHR-brehrth).

Bread is a major part of breakfast. Rye bread is very popular for both breakfast and lunch. Alternatively, people might eat *rundstykker* (rond-STOO-kehr), which are crusty rolls, or *kryddere* (KROH-dor), which are cold, toasted rolls. These are all known as *morgenbrød* (MORG-brohd), or morning breads, and are likely to be served with cheese, jam, and perhaps eggs. When the family wants a more filling breakfast, they might add cold meats and fish to the table, and pastries are often served on weekends.

Breakfast cereals have also become popular. Porridge was once the traditional Danish breakfast, and quite a few Danes still find this an agreeable way to start the day. Although Danish bacon is a popular breakfast food around the world, that is certainly not the case in Denmark. Coffee, tea, juices, and milk are the most likely breakfast drinks.

The most typical lunch consists of *smørrebrød*, or open sandwiches. These are either packed at home or bought fresh from the special *smørrebrød* shops that can be found in every neighborhood. Children frequently take *smørrebrød* for their school lunch. If the family is having lunch at home it is quite common to include a hot *smørrebrød*.

A popular alternative to *smørrebrød* is a hamburger from a fast-food stall. Although international fast-food chains are establishing a market in Denmark, they have strong competition from local brands. Small hamburger stands can be found in every town square, specializing in the high-quality Danish style of hamburger.

Danish hamburger patties are called *hakkebøf* and are made from high-quality pork. Meatballs, known as *frikadeller* (FRAHK-ah-dilehr), are a very common Danish dish, and there are numerous local recipes, such as the southern Jutland meatballs that have smoked bacon added. Fish is also quite popular in this fishing country, especially herring.

In summer, people often take their lunch down to the park or city square and enjoy a little extra time in the sunshine.

After school, children are given a small snack with milk. The main meal is eaten at about 6:00 P.M. when all the family has arrived home. Popular dishes for the main meal include pork tenderloin, hamburgers, meatballs, or herring.

As dinner is often eaten early, it is usual for Danish families to end the day with a light supper of coffee, cakes, pastry, or a small *smørrebrød* selection.

As one would expect from a nation with so much dairy produce, Denmark has produced a wonderful range of cheeses. The most famous is Danish Blue, which is quite distinctive with its blue veins and powerful taste. Other cheeses special to Denmark include Samsoe, Havarti, and Esrom.

COLD TABLE

The cold table is a very popular way of eating in Denmark and is particularly useful when unexpected guests arrive. Usually the host prepares and serves one or two warm dishes. The rest of the meal is a buffet of cold meats, vegetables, salads, cheese, and sweets. There is a selection of breads, often served heavily buttered, and herring is a favorite appetizer.

It is important to have a supply of fresh plates on hand so as not to mix the different tastes, and a good host quietly keeps all the serving plates filled.

A selection of *smørrebrod* is served on a wooden board.

THE ART OF MAKING GOOD SMØRREBRØD

If there is one food that Denmark is famous for, it is *smørrebrød*. These are open sandwiches, each one designed to be a little meal in itself.

Smørrebrød require a firm bread with a crisp crust. Although several types of bread are used, dark rye bread is by far the favorite. Getting the right size is important. Cutting the bread bigger than 2 x 4 inches (5 x 10 cm) will spoil the compact effect.

Using the correct butter is considered equally important. *Smørrebrød* literally means buttered bread, and the butter should be evenly spread without missing the edges. Butter has several jobs to perform. It is a flavoring, it stops the bread from getting soggy, and it acts as a paste to hold the toppings in place.

The list of toppings is endless, but favorites include roast beef, cheese, eel, egg, herring paté, plaice, salami, salmon, and shrimp. A typical heated *smørrebrød* would be cooked ham with egg, fried liver with onion and bacon, or fried pork with onion.

A garnish should be added, both to bring out the taste and to make it attractive to the eye; however, only one or at most two garnishes should be added to each individual sandwich.

A selection of *smørrebrød* is served together on a wooden board, but care is taken to keep the strong flavors at one end. When eating *smørrebrød*, it is polite to take only one of the little open sandwiches at a time.

DESSERTS

Most Danes enjoy rounding off a meal with a sweet dessert. Marzipan ring cakes, a nut-filled coffee cake called *kringle* (KRING-el), and layer cake are all popular.

Fruit jellies known as *rødgrød* (REHR-grehr) are another favorite desert; they are usually made from fresh fruits and homemade jelly. Depending on the season, *rødgrød* might be served with raspberries, black currants, strawberries, or rhubarb. Danes prepare an apple cake flavored with almonds and lemons and topped with thick cream.

Denmark is known for its excellent cheeses.

PASTRIES

Danish pastries—rich, flaky, sweet rolls—are famous all over the world. They are generally eaten with breakfast or as a snack.

The Danish hotdog, traditionally the most popular street food, was a hotdog in a roll, bought from a *pølsevogn*, or sausage-cart. Thirty years ago these little carts would be found on most busy streets, but today they are far less common.

Turkish and Italian restaurants now offer alternative snacks, and international fast-food chains have taken a share of the market. The traditional sausages can still be bought but are more likely to come from a service station or grocery store.

Having drinks at a street-side cafe is a popular way to spend an afternoon.

DRINKS

The two drinks that best capture the spirit of Denmark are coffee and beer. Danes are great coffee drinkers, and most people expect their coffee to come from freshly ground beans. Milk is usually added, and perhaps sugar, depending on the individual's taste. Coffee is the most likely drink for breakfast, and morning and afternoon breaks. Children are generally not encouraged to drink coffee but are more likely to drink tea or milk.

Denmark is also famous for making beer, and the Danes as a nation drink a great deal of what they produce. Some people even joke that drinking beer is part of their Viking legacy. According to one legend, the cry of *skål* (skohl) comes from Viking times when warriors drank from the skulls of their dead opponents after a battle! However, the Danish fondness for beer probably has its roots in the 16th and 17th centuries, when everybody drank weak beer because so much of the country's water supply was unsafe. Today the most popular beer is a light lager, served very cold.

Snaps (shnaps) is another traditional Danish drink. It is quite different from the German schnapps; Danish *snaps* is an alcoholic drink made from potato or barley and flavored with caraway or other herbs. It is served ice cold and drunk quickly, not sipped. You would not expect to drink *snaps* with hot food, but it is common for adults to have a snaps with cold snacks of herring or cheese.

DRINKING IN DENMARK

People are now starting to question the amount of beer being drunk in Denmark. What particularly worries and embarrasses many people is the amount of beer drunk in public. It is not unusual for people at work to share a case of beer during their breaks, or for a group of people to nonchalantly drink from bottles as they stroll down the streets.

Although there is some pressure to change this image, the strong Danish belief in individual freedom makes it difficult to enforce restrictions. Nevertheless, some firms are now banning alcohol during work hours, and a few public areas have become alcohol-free zones.

Danes joke that the only word of their language recognized throughout the world is the drinking toast skål. *This ritual way of toasting friends and guests is an important part of Danish culture.*

SKÅL

When people gather together around the table, no one starts drinking until the host or hostess has officially welcomed everybody. To do so they lift their glass, make eye contact with the guests, and say *"skål!"* This toast is then repeated by everybody at the table, with everyone raising and lowering their glasses together. There is then a third, less formal round of toasts, after which people are free to start the meal.

INFLUENCES ON DANISH FOOD

The modern Danish diet has been influenced by trends and events that can be traced back several hundred years. At the heart of Danish cuisine is the tradition of farmhouse cooking. One example of this influence is the popularity of soup. Even today, with the availability of modern convenience foods, many Danish people still prefer to make their own homemade soups. In doing so people are using recipes developed many years ago to take advantage of ingredients that were plentiful on Danish farms, such as chicken, oxtail, and vegetables. Danish soups often have small dumplings, meatballs, or vegetables floating in them.

Denmark's long tradition as a fishing nation also influences the modern diet. Herring holds a special place in Danish cooking and is eaten at just about any time of day.

Danish eating habits have changed rapidly in recent years. Both Danes traveling overseas and immigrants coming to Denmark have introduced new ideas. It is now likely for a Danish family to cook spaghetti at home or go to an Indian restaurant for a meal. Wine has also become far more popular than beer.

Like people in the rest of Europe, many Danes have become more concerned about eating healthy food and have often turned to Italian and Mediterranean dishes for ideas. However, popular Danish chefs have also drawn ideas from Danish cuisine, using local products and cooking techniques in more imaginative and healthy ways.

In the past Danes did not often eat at restaurants, largely because high taxes made eating out expensive. However, this attitude is changing. Young educated people seem far more willing to spend money on a good meal, while the opening of Turkish, Asian, and Middle Eastern restaurants have provided more opportunities to eat out on a lower budget.

SPECIAL CARE IN SETTING THE TABLE

Danish china, table linen, and tableware are among the finest in the world, and most homes have a varied collection of table settings for creating different atmospheres. Danish people are likely to decorate the table for most evening meals and not just on special occasions.

In a country where the seasons affect the lifestyle so much, flowers play a special role as table decorations. In addition to those bought at the florist, wildflowers and grasses are picked during summer. In autumn dried flowers bring the browns and golds of the season into the room, and even in the dark months after Christmas a tiny display of snowdrops or crocuses often brightens the table.

Candles are also used to add light and warmth to the room and contribute to the special *hygge* atmosphere.

THE DANISH KITCHEN

The Danish kitchen is a very important part of the house and brings out the best in Danish design. Real-estate agents attempting to sell a house often use pictures of the kitchen to attract buyers. A typical Danish feature is to have an open design where the kitchen and dining room are separated only by a low wall.

OPEN SANDWICHES

Use sliced wholegrain bread as the base of the sandwich. If you use white bread, toast first. Butter the bread before adding the toppings. The toppings listed below are typical. Start with the fish and then go on to the meat. Danes often finish with a *smørrebrød* of cheese on white bread.

1. Take a bottle of pickled herring and drain the fish. Cut into small pieces and place on the bread. Decorate with slices of green pepper, onion, and tomato.
2. Mix small shrimps with mayonnaise and dill weed. Spread on the bread, and decorate with a small piece of twisted lemon.
3. Cover the bread with liver paste, and add bacon, tomato, beetroot, and horseradish. This is called the "Hans Christian Andersen," because it is a favorite with Danish children.
4. Cover the bread with slices of cheese. Mix shrimp with mayonnaise, and spread over the cheese. Decorate with parsley.
5. Spread scrambled eggs on the bread, and put a little smoked salmon in the center. Decorate with parsley.
6. Thinly slice a hard-boiled egg. Place on the bread along with anchovies.

A dollop of mayonnaise and mustard sauce can be used as the final dressing or as the base instead of butter. To make this sauce, mix 1 cup mayonnaise, 4 teaspoons mustard, 1 tablespoon chopped capers, 4 tablespoons chopped chives, and a pinch of salt and pepper in a bowl until smooth. Refrigerate for an hour before use.

STRAWBERRY PUDDING

Strawberries are a great summer favorite in Denmark. This is a very typical and easy recipe.

2 pounds (910 g) strawberries
1 cup sugar
enough water to cover the strawberries
$\frac{1}{2}$ cup cornstarch
1–2 teaspoons vanilla extract

Rinse the strawberries, place in water, and bring to a boil. Add the sugar and let the strawberries simmer for about 10 minutes until tender. Mix the cornstarch with a little water, and slowly stir into the strawberry mixture. The resulting pudding should be quite fluid and not lumpy. Add the vanilla and boil for three more minutes. Leave to cool, and then sprinkle with sugar and serve with cream. Danes sometimes like to mix the cream with a little milk.

A   **B**   **C**   **D**

Streymoy

● Tórshavn

FAEROE
ISLANDS

NORWAY

1

Skagerrak

Skagen ●

2

● Frederikshavn

Læsø

S W E D E N

N

● Ålborg

Kattegat

Løgstør
Bredning
Lim Fjord

**NORTHERN
JUTLAND**

3

VIBORG

Randers Fjord

Gudenå

ÅRHUS

J u t l a n d

Århus ●

Øresund

RINGKØBING

Ringkøbing
Fjord

Skjern

Yding Skovhøj
(568 ft / 170 m) ▲

Arresø

Roskilde Fjord

**FREDERIKS-
BORG**

● Billund

● Jelling

VEJLE

Samsø

**WEST
ZEALAND**

Isle Fjord

Gentofte ●
Frederiksberg ● COPENHAGEN

RIBE

● Fredericia

Odense
Fjord

Z e a l a n d

Roskilde ●

COPENHAGEN

● Esbjerg

Fanø

● Odense

Store Bælt

Amager

ROSKILDE

4

Ribe ●

Lille Bælt

FYN

**SOUTHERN
JUTLAND**

Als

STORSTRØM

Møn

BALTIC

Bornholm

Aerø

Falster

Langeland

Lolland

SEA

5

*NORTH

SEA*

**SCHLESWIG-
HOLSTEIN**

G E R M A N Y

● Capital city
● Major town
▲ Mountain peak

Feet	Meters
16,500	5,000
9,900	3,000
6,600	2,000
3,300	1,000
1,650	500
660	200
0	0

MAP OF DENMARK

ECONOMIC DENMARK

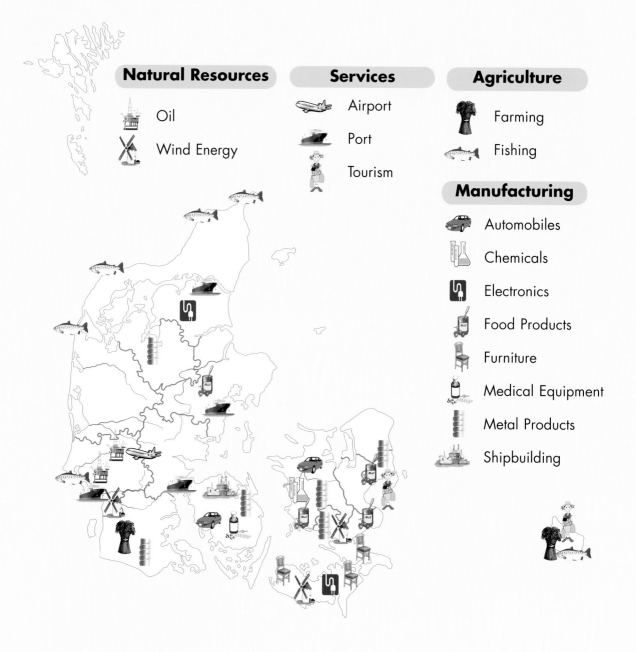

Natural Resources
- Oil
- Wind Energy

Services
- Airport
- Port
- Tourism

Agriculture
- Farming
- Fishing

Manufacturing
- Automobiles
- Chemicals
- Electronics
- Food Products
- Furniture
- Medical Equipment
- Metal Products
- Shipbuilding

ABOUT THE ECONOMY

OVERVIEW
Despite having limited mineral resources, Denmark has become one of the world's wealthiest nations. Denmark imports many of its basic materials, while its exports consist mostly of high-quality manufactured products.

GROSS DOMESTIC PRODUCT (GDP)
$174.4 billion (2004 estimate)

GDP BY SECTOR
Agriculture 2.2 percent, industry 25.5 percent, services 72.3 percent (2004 estimate)

LAND AREA
16,639 square miles (43,094 square km); 54 percent is arable land.

AGRICULTURAL PRODUCTS
Cereals, potatoes, pork, dairy products, fish

INFLATION RATE
1.4 percent (2004 estimate)

CURRENCY
1 Danish kroner (DKK) = 100 ore
USD 1 = DKK 6 (September 2005)
Notes: 50, 100, 200, 500 and 1,000 kroner
Coins: 25, 50 øre; 1, 2, 5, 10, 20 kroner

WORKFORCE
2.87 million (2004 estimate)

UNEMPLOYMENT RATE
6.2 percent (2004 estimate)

INDUSTRIAL PRODUCTS
Iron, steel, ships, transportation equipment, chemicals, food products, textiles, electronics, furniture, wood products, windmills

PORTS AND HARBORS
Åbenraa, Ålborg, Århus, Copenhagen, Esbjerg, Fredericia, Kolding, Odense, Roenne (Bornholm), Vejle

MAJOR EXPORTS
Machinery, dairy and meat products, ships, fish, chemicals, windmills

MAJOR IMPORTS
Machinery, petroleum, chemicals, food products, textiles, paper

MAJOR TRADE PARTNERS
Germany, Sweden, United Kingdom, United States, Norway, France, the Netherlands, Italy

AIRPORTS
Copenhagen and Billund are the largest.

MAIN INTERNATIONAL PARTICIPATION
European Union (EU), United Nations (UN), North Atlantic Treaty Organization (NATO)

CULTURAL DENMARK

Jelling
Jelling has a unique collection of burial mounds and runic stones from pre-Christian Denmark. A UNESCO World Heritage Site.

Århus
A university city noted for music and entertainment. It has a famous open-air museum with restored buildings gathered from all over Denmark.

Skagen
Made famous in the 1800s when Denmark's leading artists came here to paint in the beautiful light. Skagens Museum has an excellent collection of paintings from this school.

Kronborg Castle
The dramatic Kronborg Castle guards the narrow waterway between Denmark and Sweden. Construction started in 1574, although much of the present-day castle dates to the 17th century. This was Shakespeare's setting for Hamlet.

Ribe
The oldest town in Scandinavia, dating back to A.D. 700. There is a Viking center where you can experience life in Denmark a thousand years ago.

Odense
Odense is the hometown of Hans Christian Anderson and Carl Nielsen. There are museums dedicated to both men.

Copenhagen
Copenhagen is the center of Danish culture. You can visit the National Museum to see the rich collection of Danish historical material, watch a ballet, or listen to an opera.

Tivoli Gardens
An amusement park and garden in the heart of Copenhagen. It opens from mid-April through mid-September when there is a daily program of concerts and entertainment. It reopens for a few weeks before Christmas for a market and ice-skating.

Little Mermaid
Based on the Hans Christian Anderson fairy story, the Little Mermaid is one of the most famous statues in Europe and has sat in the Copenhagen harbor since 1913.

Legoland
A theme park in Billund made out of 42 million pieces of the famous plastic toy building bricks.

Roskilde
Roskilde is famous for its Viking ship museum, its cathedral, and its annual music festival.

ABOUT THE CULTURE

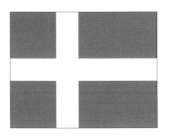

OFFICIAL NAME
Kongeriget Danmark (Kingdom Of Denmark)

NATIONAL FLAG
Red with a white cross

NATIONAL ANTHEM
Der er et yndigt land (*There is a Lovely Land*)

CAPITAL
Copenhagen

OTHER MAJOR CITIES
Århus, Odense, Ålborg

ETHNIC GROUPS
Danish, other Scandinavians, Asians, Turkish residents of the former Yugloslavia, Africans

RELIGIOUS GROUPS
Evangelical Lutheran Christian 95 percent, Muslim 2 percent, Roman Catholic and other Christian 3 percent

MIGRATION RATE
2.53 per 1,000 (2004 estimate)

OFFICIAL LANGUAGE
Danish. English is widely spoken as a second language.

LITERACY RATE
100 percent

INTERNET USERS
3.72 million (2005 estimate)

TIME
Central European Time: Greenwich Mean Time plus one hour (GMT/UTC + 0100)

IMPORTANT ANNIVERSARIES
Referendum in Southern Jutland (February 10), Occupation of Denmark (April 9), Liberation of Denmark (May 5)

LEADERS IN POLITICS
Anders Fogh Rasmussen—prime minister since 2001
Queen Margrethe II—head of state since 1972
Crown Prince Frederik—heir to the throne

FAMOUS DANES
Carl Nielsen (composer), Hans Christian Andersen (writer), Niels Bohr (physicist), Karen Blixen (author), Bertel Thorvaldsen (artist), A.P. Møller (industrialist), Kim Larsen (pop musician), Lars von Trier (film director), Morten Olsen (soccer coach), Anders Hejlsberg (developed computer languages), Jens Christian Skou (chemist and Nobel Prize winner), Bille August (film director), Brian and Michael Laudrup (soccer players)

TIME LINE

IN DENMARK	IN THE WORLD
12,500–12,000 B.C.	
Humans follow reindeer herds into Denmark.	
3900–1700 B.C.	
First evidence of people growing crops and keeping livestock	**753 B.C.**
	Rome is founded.
	116–17 B.C.
	The Roman Empire reaches its greatest extent,
A.D. 0–400	under Emperor Trajan (98–17).
Evidence of trade with the Roman empire	
	A.D. 600
800	Height of Mayan civilization
Start of the Viking period	
883	
King Gorm becomes the first known ruler of a Danish kingdom.	
965	
Harald Bluetooth claims all of Denmark and converts the country to Christianity.	**1000**
1013	The Chinese perfect gunpowder and
Denmark and England are united.	begin to use it in warfare.
1397	
Queen Margrethe achieves union between Denmark, Sweden, and Norway.	
1523	
Sweden elects Gustav Vasa as king. Norway remains under Danish rule.	**1530**
1536	Beginning of trans-Atlantic slave trade organized by the Portuguese in Africa.
Danish Lutheran Church is established.	**1558–1603**
1618–48	Reign of Elizabeth I of England
Denmark fights in the Thirty Years War.	
	1776
1788	U.S. Declaration of Independence
Stavnsbaand, the custom that binds farmers to the land, is abolished.	**1789–99**
	The French Revolution
1801–07	
British navy attacks Copenhagen.	**1861**
	The U.S. Civil War begins.

IN DENMARK	IN THE WORLD
	1869 The Suez Canal is opened.
1886 Prussia takes Schleswig and Holstein.	**1914** World War I begins.
1915 First parliament elected by universal suffrage.	
1920 North Schleswig is returned to Denmark.	**1939** World War II begins.
1940 Nazi Germany invades.	
1944 Iceland declares independence.	
1945 German occupation ends.	**1945** The United States drops atomic bombs on Hiroshima and Nagasaki.
1948 Faeroe Islands gain home rule.	**1949** The North Atlantic Treaty Organization (NATO) is formed.
	1957 The Russians launch Sputnik.
	1966–69 The Chinese Cultural Revolution
1973 Denmark joins the European Community.	
1979 Greenland is given home rule.	**1986** Nuclear power disaster at Chernobyl in Ukraine
	1991 Break-up of the Soviet Union
1993 Danes accept the Maastricht Treaty with conditions.	**1997** Hong Kong is returned to China.
2000 Danes reject the euro.	
2001 Anders Fogh Rasmussen becomes prime minister and leads a right-wing coalition government.	**2001** Terrorists crash planes in New York, Washington, D.C., and Pennsylvania.
	2003 War in Iraq

GLOSSARY

Danelaw
Region in western England that was colonized by the Vikings.

Evangelical Lutheran
Christian denomination that follows the beliefs of the Reformation and traces its history to Martin Luther.

Fastelvn (fasta-laon)
The holiday preceding Lent.

fjord
A large inlet from the sea.

folkeskole (fol-kes-skohla)
A combined elementary and junior high school.

Folketing
Danish parliament.

frikadeller (FRACK-ah-dil-er)
Meatballs.

hygge (hoo-ga)
A feeling of warmth and coziness.

Inuit
Native peoples of Greenland.

Maastricht Treaty
Treaty signed on February 7, 1992, between the members of the European Community. It led to the formation of the European Union.

morgenbrød (MOHRG-brohd)
Literally, morning bread; a type of bread served at breakfast with cheese or jam.

Nisse (NISS-ah)
Elf-like creatures from Danish folklore, now commonly associated with Christmas.

North Atlantic Drift
Warm current from the Gulf of Mexico that moderates Denmark's cold climate.

rejsegilde (RAI-seh-gilder)
Traditional Danish ceremony to celebrate the completion of a new house.

rigsdansk (rihj-dansk)
Standard spoken Danish, used by newscasters.

roligans (ROHL-ee-gans)
From the Danish *rolig* (calm) and the English "hooligans." Applied to Danish soccer fans.

Scandinavia
The four northern European countries: Denmark, Sweden, Norway, and Finland.

skål (skohl)
Danish drinking toast.

wattle and daub
Frame of woven tree branches covered with a paste of straw, mud, and cow dung, used by the Vikings for house walls.

FURTHER INFORMATION

BOOKS

Bender, Andrew, Sally O'Brien, Andrew Stone, and Michael Grosberg. *Lonely Planet Denmark*. Melbourne, Australia: Lonely Planet Publications, 2005.

Jespersen, Knud J. V. *A History of Denmark*. New York: Palgrave Macmillan, 2004.

Shakespeare, William. *Hamlet, Prince of Denmark*. The New Cambridge Shakepeare Series. Cambridge University Press, 2003.

WEB SITES

Central Intelligence Agency World Factbook (select Denmark from the country list). www.cia.gov/cia/publications/factbook

Danish Environment Protection Agency. www.mst.dk/homepage

Danish Ministry of Foreign Affairs. www.um.dk

Danish Tourist Board. www.visitdenmark.com

Denmark official website. www.denmark.dk

Embassy of Denmark in Washington. www.denmarkemb.org

Nordic Shop: Denmark. www.scandinavia.com/denmark.htm

UNESCO World Heritage Centre. http://whc.unesco.org

Wikipedia: Denmark. http://wikipedia.org/wiki/Denmark

World Recipes: Denmark. www.world-recipes.info/denmark-danish

MUSIC

Kim Larsen and Kjukken. EMI, 1996.

Nielsen: The Symphonies (Nos. 1–3). San Francisco Symphony. Conducted by Herbert Blomstedt. Decca, 1999.

VIDEOS

Babette's Feast. Directed by Gabriel Axel. MGM, 1987.

Miss Smilla's Sense of Snow. Directed by Bille August. Twentieth Century Fox, 1997.

Help! I'm a Fish. Directed by Stefan Fjeldmark and Michael Hegner. Prism Leisure Corporation. 2003.

BIBLIOGRAPHY

Best, Beth Wagner. *The Amazing Paper Cuttings of Hans Christian Andersen.* New York: Ticknor and Fields, 1991.

Hintz, Martin. *Denmark.* Chicago: Children's Press, 1994.

Hull, Robert. *Norse Stories.* New York: Thomsen Learning, 1993.

Lerner Publications. *Denmark—In Pictures.* Minneapolis, MN: Lerner Publications, 1991.

Odijk, Pamela. *The Vikings.* Englewood Cliffs, NJ: Silver Burdett, 1990.

INDEX